Praise for *The Happy Herbivore Cookbook*

"An exciting collection of healthy and delectable vegan dishes."
—Mark Reinfeld, coauthor of *The 30-Minute Vegan, The Complete Idiots Guide to Eating Raw,* **and** *Vegan Fusion World Cuisine*

"The Happy Herbivore Cookbook proves how delicious, easy, and accessible low-fat vegan food can be."
—Alicia C. Simpson, author of *Quick and Easy Vegan Comfort Food*

"The Happy Herbivore Cookbook is a treasury of healthy, delicious dishes that are sure to please even the pickiest of eaters. With a wide variety of easy recipes, Nixon shows how truly sumptuous vegan meals can be."
—Susan Voisin, founder of FatfreeVegan.com

"The Happy Herbivore Cookbook is easy to read and filled with simple-to-prepare and delicious healthy recipes. We recommend that you make this part of your kitchen library. Using it often will help you preserve (and regain) your health and appearance."
—John and Mary McDougall, founders of the McDougall Program

"The Happy Herbivore Cookbook will not only make all your culinary dreams come true but will give you a recipe for lifelong health. Lindsay Nixon's recipes are not just vegan but also low in fat, which our research at the Physicians Committee for Responsible Medicine has proven to be a winning combination for disease prevention and reversal. The only danger with this book is reading it on an empty stomach, as all the recipes will be calling your name—like Cajun Home Fries, Mushroom Burgers, Fettuccine Alfredo, Baked Onion Rings, and Root Beer Float Cupcakes. Nixon not only offers expertise on how to cook delicious vegan food, she shows you how to shop and gives you pantry suggestions, ideas for substitutions, plenty of variations, and nutrient analysis for each recipe. So, jump on in, get your feet wet with all the foods you thought you'd have to set aside to get healthy— delicious vegan food is here and yours for the taking. May you be the happiest and healthiest Herbivore with Nixon's culinary expertise."
—Neal Barnard, president, Physicians Committee for Responsible Medicine

*"*Sure, a plant-based diet is often touted as healthier than the Standard American Diet, but 'vegan' doesn't automatically translate to 'low-fat'—and no one knows this better than Lindsay Nixon. In her new cookbook, Nixon offers up a wide array of tried-and-true favorites made over. Recipes range from vegan classics like Chili sans Carne to Macaroni and 'Cheese,' as well as interesting twists on otherwise high-fat foods (such as the ingenious nutty spread or instant cookie dough)—you'll be amazed at how these foods can be rendered fat-free and still taste delicious. Though I don't follow a fat-free diet, *The Happy Herbivore* recipe is still the one I turn to first when I'm looking for a tofu omelet. With its fuss-free recipes and easily accessible ingredients, *The Happy Herbivore Cookbook* is an ideal cookbook for anyone just embarking on a journey to veganism as well as for those seasoned vegans who simply wish to reduce their overall fat intake."
—Ricki Heller, PhD, RHN, author of *Sweet Freedom: Desserts You'll Love without Wheat, Eggs, Dairy, or Refined Sugar*

"The Happy Herbivore Cookbook is a fantastic resource for delicious vegan recipes. Nixon's unique and healthy whole-food recipes not only taste great, they are also a wonderful tool for gaining optimum health."
—Tess Challis, vegan chef and author of *Radiant Health, Inner Wealth,* **and** *The Two-Week Wellness Solution*

"The Happy Herbivore Cookbook's low-fat, plant-based dishes promote health in a delectable and wholesome way. Lindsay Nixon's recipes are a practical and affordable means to a nutritious lifestyle that can help prevent and reverse disease. Whether one has been employing a plant-based diet for years or is just starting, *The Happy Herbivore Cookbook* gives simple and flavorful solutions to eat better for mental and physical health."
—T. Colin Campbell, PhD, professor emeritus of Nutritional Biochemistry and author of *The China Study*

The Happy Herbivore Cookbook

OVER 175 DELICIOUS FAT-FREE & LOW-FAT VEGAN RECIPES

LINDSAY S. NIXON

BenBella Books, Inc.
Dallas, Texas

BenBella Books, Inc.
10300 N. Central Expressway, Suite 400
Dallas, TX 75231
www.benbellabooks.com
Send feedback to feedback@benbellabooks.com

Printed in the United States of America
10 9 8 7

Library of Congress Cataloging-in-Publication Data is available for this title.
978-1-935618-12-6

Copyediting by Jennifer DePrima
Proofreading by Erica Lovett and Iris Bass
Cover design by Kit Sweeney
Text design and composition by Kit Sweeney
Index by Lindsay S. Nixon
Printed by Bang

Distributed by Perseus Distribution
(www.perseusdistribution.com)
To place orders through Perseus Distribution:
Tel: 800-343-4499
Fax: 800-351-5073
E-mail: orderentry@perseusbooks.com

**Significant discounts for bulk sales are available. Please contact
Glenn Yeffeth at glenn@benbellabooks.com or (214) 750-3628.**

Table of Contents

MIX & MATCH: VEGETABLES, GRAINS, & BEANS

DESSERTS

DIPS, SNACKS, & FINGER FOODS

INTRODUCTION

A Word from Lindsay

Happyherbivore.com was created as a way to bring healthy but delicious vegan food to others. This cookbook emulates that vision. Each recipe will delight anyone who tries it. You'll find yourself saying, "I can't believe it's vegan!" and "I can't believe this is healthy food!" This cookbook will proudly show you that eating healthy doesn't have to be a chore and can instead be a pleasure.

Each recipe is made with whole foods and no added fat. You won't find processed flour, refined sugars, or gobs of oil and margarine in these recipes. What you will find is food that is good for you and tastes great. You'll find muffins that are so moist you won't believe they're fat-free, and cookies and cupcakes so scrumptious you'll deny that they're healthy foods. You'll also find healthy versions of comfort foods that warm your soul but don't expand your waistline and clog your arteries. In a nutshell, you'll eat what seems like pure decadence with nothing but sweet, sweet rewards of health and vitality.

Additionally, all of the recipes have been designed to be accessible to every person, every palate, and every budget. These recipes do not use bizarre, obscure ingredients or tools. Rather, they use ordinary, inexpensive ingredients you always have on hand and everyday cookware. Most of the recipes are also quick and easy to whip up and can be made without a special trip to the grocery store.

Why Vegan?

Eating a plant-based diet is the nation's fastest-growing food trend, and for good reason. The more plant-based meals we eat, the more benefits we will feel and bestow. Adopting a plant-based diet is the single best thing we can do for our health, our wallets, the environment, humanity, and farm animals everywhere. Anytime someone asks me why I'm a vegan, I reply, "For my health, the animals, the environment, my pocketbook . . . and for you."

HEALTH: A vegan diet has zero dietary cholesterol, and a low-fat vegan diet also tends to be low in calories but high in fiber. Some studies have also shown that eating a low-fat vegan diet can prevent, cure, and reverse devastating diseases like hypertension, diabetes, and cancer.

WALLETS: A vegan diet can be a bargain. Vegan staples like beans, rice, and non-dairy milks cost a fraction of the price of meats and dairy products. Plus, eating healthfully will save you on health care costs in the long run.

ENVIRONMENT: A vegan diet is the most eco-friendly and sustainable way we can eat.

HUMANITY: It has been said that if the world went vegetarian, we would almost immediately end world hunger. One acre of land can produce either 20,000 pounds of potatoes or a measly 165 pounds of meat.

ANIMALS: The lives and deaths of farm animals are often horrifyingly brutal, both physically and psychologically. As a consumer picking up the end product, it's easy to be oblivious rather than conscious.

MY STORY I was a vegetarian for most of my childhood out of a love for animals—I was eating a burger one day in the car as we drove past grazing cows and when I put it together, that was that. But I fell into a meat-eating lifestyle in my teens out of peer pressure. A serious health scare in my early twenties brought me back to a vegetarian diet, and then I went vegan the following year as an experiment.

After reading *The China Study*, *Eat to Live*, and *Skinny Bitch* I knew I could never go back to vegetarianism. I made my vegan regimen permanent as well as a new addition: a diet that not only cut out meat, dairy, and eggs, but one that was low-fat and based on whole foods.

I noticed positive changes instantly. I lost weight, going from 160 pounds to 135, from a size 12 to a size 4. I also had fewer migraines and generally felt happier and less stressed. I also noticed an increase in my energy levels. In fact, I had so much energy that I ran a marathon ten months after adopting a low-fat vegan diet without so much as having run a 5K before!

Why Fat-Free and Low-Fat?

Like many other Americans, my husband and I both struggled with our weight and health for years. After I read *The China Study: The Most Comprehensive Study of Nutrition Ever Conducted and the Startling Implications for Diet, Weight Loss, and Long-term Health*; *The McDougall Program: 12 Days to Dynamic Health*; and *Eat to Live: The Revolutionary Plan for Fast and Sustained Weight Loss*, I adopted a low-fat, no-added-fat vegan diet, and my husband joined me shortly thereafter. In the span of a year, we both lost more weight than we previously thought possible. Our general health also improved. I no longer had acne and migraines, while my husband reversed his early-onset IBS. We also noticed a surge in our energy levels and went on to complete our first marathons and adopt athletic activities such as snowboarding, rock climbing, and mountain biking—sports that never seemed realistic or possible before.

Most added fats, including oils, are dangerous to our health. We all know about the risks and dangers of hydrogenated fats, but other fats, like extra-virgin olive oil, are also harmful when heated. Most "cooking oils," such as canola, olive, corn, and peanut, have very low burning points. When they are heated beyond that boiling point, either by sautéing food, baking it in the oven, or deep frying food in oil, the nutrients in the oil are lost. This makes the oil a high-calorie and high-fat food, yet one without any nutrients. In other words, the oils are empty calories. Worse still, heating oils beyond their boiling points causes free radicals to be created. The only oils that can stand to be heated at high temperatures are coconut oil, sunflower oil, and safflower oil.

Cold-pressed oils that are not heated may retain their nutrients, but because they're processed, they have little nutrition and they still have fat; for example, 1 tablespoon of oil has approximately 14 grams of fat—the same as a candy bar!

To obtain essential fatty acids, enjoy whole, unprocessed fats, such as nuts, seeds, coconuts, and avocados, sparingly. Also remember that a lot of foods, including legumes, naturally contain a little fat. This means the body is always getting plenty of fat without your adding extra.

Getting Started

Most of the ingredients in this cookbook can be found in any supermarket, but a select few will require a trip to the health food store or placing an order online if you prefer. If you are new to vegan food, whole foods, or low-fat cooking, some of the ingredients in this cookbook might be new to you, so check the Glossary of Ingredients (pg. 287) to learn about them and where you can find them for the lowest price.

SHOPPING LIST

Below is my basic shopping list. If you have these ingredients on hand you can make almost anything in this cookbook without making a special trip to the grocery store. I highly recommend buying low-sodium and/or no-salt-added items whenever possible, particularly with canned goods such as tomatoes or beans, soy sauce, and vegetable broth. I also recommend selecting organic and unsweetened varieties and avoiding items that contain refined sugar, high-fructose corn syrup, fat (particularly hydrogenated fats), and anything that's not vegan (contains dairy, meat, eggs, fish, or animal by-products such as gelatin, casein, or whey).

PANTRY:

agave nectar	garlic	sweet potatoes or yams
baking powder	high-heat cooking spray (such	Tetra-packed shelf-stable tofu
baking soda	as coconut or safflower)	such as Mori-Nu tofu
balsamic vinegar	instant oats	textured vegetable protein
brown rice	marinara sauce	(TVP) or textured soy
brown rice flour	mirin or sherry	protein (TSP)
brown sugar	non-dairy milks	tomato sauce
canned tomatoes	old-fashioned rolled oats	tomato paste
canned green chilies	onions	unsweetened applesauce
canned pure pumpkin	pure maple syrup	unsweetened cocoa
chickpea flour	quinoa	vegetable broth and/or
confectioners' sugar	raw sugar	vegetable bouillon cubes
distilled white vinegar	roasted red peppers (in water,	vanilla extract
dried fruits such as raisins	not oil)	vital wheat gluten
and cranberries	russet or Idaho potatoes	whole-wheat or brown rice pasta
dried and/or canned beans	salsas (variety)	whole-wheat breadcrumbs
dried lentils and split peas	smooth peanut butter	yellow cornmeal

REFRIGERATOR:

barbecue sauce
carrots
celery
corn tortillas
Dijon mustard
firm and extra-firm tofu
hot sauce
ketchup
lemon juice

lettuce or salad mixes
lime juice
low-sodium soy sauce or
    tamari
non-dairy milks
nutritional yeast
prepared yellow mustard
seasonal fresh fruits and
    vegetables

soy yogurt or other plain
    non-dairy yogurt
steak sauce
vegan Parmesan cheese
vegan cream cheese
whole-wheat or sprouted
    bread, pitas, and tortillas
yellow miso paste

FREEZER:

frozen berries and fruits
leafy greens such as spinach
    or turnip greens

mixed vegetables such as
    stir-fry mixed vegetables
peeled bananas
raw nuts and seeds (optional)

whole-wheat buns and breads
whole-wheat pastry flour
yellow corn

SPICES:

bay leaves
black pepper
cayenne powder
chili powder
chipotle powder
ground coriander
dried marjoram and/or
    oregano
dried minced onion or
    onion flakes

dried rosemary
dried thyme
fennel seeds
garam masla
granulated garlic powder
ground cinnamon
ground cumin
ground nutmeg
iodized fine sea salt
Italian seasoning

kelp granules
mild curry powder
granulated onion powder
paprika
pumpkin pie spice
red pepper flakes
rubbed sage (not powdered)
turmeric

Tools are important, too. You'll need pots and pans, a sharp knife, mixing bowls, measuring cups and spoons, at least one cutting board, a baking sheet, a whisk and spatula, a strainer, grater, and a food processor or blender. Optional: a toaster oven, a garlic press, a flat-iron pan, an electric steamer, and a microwave.

Kitchen Prep Lingo

I remember my early days in the kitchen. They were filled with questions like, "How small is a small onion?" or "What is the difference between mince and chop?" To help cut back on your Google searches, I've created this cheat sheet of terms you'll run across in this cookbook.

ALMOST COMBINED/JUST COMBINED: Do not completely combine ingredients. With batter, some flour should still be visible for it to be almost combined. To be just combined, stir it just a little bit more—ingredients should be mixed together and are incorporated but barely. Use as few strokes as possible. (Compare with Blend, below.)

BANANAS—RIPENESS AND SIZE: Unripe bananas are completely green. Barely ripe bananas have some yellow but are green at the ends. Ripe bananas are yellow and lightly spotted. Very ripe bananas are very spotted but not mostly or completely brown. Brown bananas are overly ripe. A medium or average banana is approximately eight inches long. Anything smaller is considered a small banana, and anything over nine inches is considered a large or extra-large banana. Use a medium, ripe banana unless the recipe specifies otherwise.

BEANS: Use canned beans, drained and rinsed, unless the recipe specifically calls for dried beans.

BLANCHING: A cooking technique that involves tossing vegetables into boiling water very briefly and then immediately chilling them in ice water so the vegetables stop cooking and remain crisp and tender.

BLEND: Stirring to incorporate all ingredients until they are well combined and the mix is homogenous. (Also called Whiz.)

CHOP: Cut ingredient into bite-sized pieces; uniform cuts are not necessary, and size is relatively unimportant (it's more of a personal preference).

COOKED: A vegetable prepared by steaming, baking, or boiling until fork-tender and seeded and/or skinned prior to cooking if necessary.

CREAM: Beat the ingredients with an electric mixer until well combined and they have a creamy consistency. This also can be done by hand with a spatula.

CRUMBLE: Break ingredient apart into smaller pieces. With tofu, break the tofu apart until it resembles ricotta or feta cheese.

DICE: Chop the ingredient into uniform cubes, approximately half an inch.

FOLD: Gently stir a single ingredient into a mixture, such as muffin batter, with a spatula or large spoon until just combined.

GREASE: Lightly spray a pot, pan, paper liner, or other container with cooking spray. If you don't have a cooking spray can, add a tiny dab of oil into the center and use a clean napkin, paper towel, or rubber spatula to spread the oil around, making a thin layer along all surfaces.

LINE: Add a thin layer of water or broth that just barely covers the bottom of the pot or skillet. Start with ¼ cup of liquid.

MINCE: Chop ingredients into very small pieces one–eighth inch or smaller.

ONION: Small onions are the size of a lemon, medium onions are roughly the size of an orange, and large onions are the size of a grapefruit.

PACKED TIGHT: Completely filling the measuring container without a lot of air to help fill the space.

PRESS: Drain tofu, then wrap it in a clean paper towel. Place it between two cutting boards or a cookie sheet and cutting board, with the board on top. Place something heavy on top, such as a 28-ounce can of tomatoes. Allow the weight to press excess water out of the tofu for at least twenty minutes. After it's been pressed, pat dry with a clean paper towel. (Nasoya also makes an inexpensive tofu press machine.)

SALT AND PEPPER TO TASTE: ½ teaspoon salt and ¼ teaspoon pepper is usually a good starting point for recipes that serve at least two. Reduce salt if you're using ingredients with sodium, such as canned goods or soy sauce. Double spices as necessary to achieve your preferred taste.

SEASON TO TASTE: The same as salt and pepper to taste.

SKILLET: Also known as a frying pan; generally, you'll want to use a medium or large skillet.

SPRINKLE: Scatter an ingredient lightly over the top.

STIR: Use a circular motion, clockwise or counterclockwise, to move or incorporate ingredients.

WHIZ: Another word for Blending.

Troubleshooting Tips

Always spoon your flour into your measuring cup lightly and gently. Scooping flour out of the bag or eyeballing your measurement will lead you astray by about two ounces. Any overages in flour will result in dense baked goods or other failures.

Be careful about how many changes and adaptations you make in a recipe. When making a change or substitution, think about the big picture and ask yourself, "What does that ingredient do?" Some recipes can handle a lot of substitutions and adaptations, others cannot.

To prevent sticking, use nonstick pans or parchment paper, or lightly grease your pan before baking. If you are using paper cups, be sure to spray the liners with a cooking spray first.

Know your oven temperature and find where the hot spots are by using an oven thermometer.

When adapting a recipe to fat-free, try not to bake at more than 350°F regardless of what the original recipe states. Your baked goods may burn or dry out at a higher temperature with the fats removed.

Key baking ingredients such as baking powder and baking soda cannot be substituted or swapped. It is also recommended you do not increase or decrease the specified amount.

Allow the baked goods to cool fully before trying to peel the liners off.

Gently stir the batter until just combined unless the directions state otherwise. Overstirring or whipping the batter intensely will negatively affect the end result of your baked goods; it might, for example, make it too dense, gummy, or doughy, or it could fail to rise completely.

Baking pans change cooking times. Be mindful of what baking pan you are using. Is it a regular, nonstick, glass, or dark pan?

How to Use This Book

 NO COOKING REQUIRED: Recipes that don't require any cooking or require very minimal passive cooking, such as toasting bread.

 QUICK: Recipes that can be made, start to finish, in 30 minutes or less. Some recipes may require multitasking to complete in 30 minutes.

 FAT-FREE: Recipes with less than 1 gram of fat per serving.

 GLUTEN-FREE: Recipes that don't require whole-wheat flours, vital wheat gluten, seitan, or barley. I can't vouch for all the ingredients, so if you have an allergy, please make sure every ingredient you use (e.g., soy sauce, spices, or oats) is a certified gluten free brand. You can also substitute tamari for soy sauce.

 SOY-FREE: Recipes that don't require tofu, soy sauce, TVP (textured vegetable/soy protein), or other soy products. If the recipe calls for non-dairy milk, you can make it soy-free by using almond, hemp, or rice milk, or another soy-free option.

 KID-FRIENDLY: Recipes that went over especially well with my testers' children.

 OMNI-FRIENDLY: All of the recipes in this book have been taste tested by vegans and omnivores alike, but recipes with this icon were the meat-eaters' favorites, making them perfect for mixed-diet gatherings.

Top Ten Tips

1 Before starting, read each recipe thoroughly, paying close attention to the directions and looking up unfamiliar ingredients in the Glossary of Ingredients (pg. 287) and unfamiliar methods in the Kitchen Prep Lingo section (pg. 6).

2 Clean a space where you can work. Make sure the pots and pans and other tools you'll need are clean and set them up if necessary. Next, gather all of the ingredients and prep them as directed. Having everything right at your fingertips before you begin is invaluable.

3 Don't hold recipes captive. Worry about perfect precision only when you're baking. A little more or less of a spice will not make or break a recipe.

4 Always spoon your flour into your measuring cup lightly and gently; never scoop it out of the bag.

5 Know your oven temperature and locate the hot spots using an oven thermometer.

6 If you're new to vegan food, start with recipes that are inherently vegetarian, like veggie-laden dishes, and work your way up to tofu and meat substitutes (also called meat analogues, meat replacements, or mock meats; see Vegan Meats in the glossary).

7 If you're new to low-fat cooking, start with a dessert recipe or comfort food dish and be sure to include the optional ingredients.

8 If you make an adaption or substitution, think about the big picture and ask yourself: "What does that ingredient do? Is it essential? Does my substitution look, taste, weigh, feel, and have the same moisture and texture as the original ingredient?"

9 Keep an open mind. If you think something will taste amazing, it probably will. If you go into a new recipe with a bad attitude, you'll likely have a bad experience.

10 Relax and have fun—keeping Zen in the kitchen is every chef's best-kept secret for awesome results (I listen to music to keep the peace).

RECIPES

Breakfast & Brunch

Frittata G 🕐

Serves 6 | Pictured opposite and on pg. 12 | By definition, a frittata is an Italian omelet made with cheese, meat, vegetables, or pasta, but in vegan terms it's just a baked tofu scramble. (Though "frittata" sounds so much sexier.) This is my basic frittata recipe, and it's meant to be played with by adding any leftover vegetables or other ingredients that you have on hand. My favorite addition is ½ cup of chopped fresh dill, but I also like to add mushrooms, spinach, tomato, and fresh basil or vegetarian meats. Cleaning out the fridge has never been so tasty!

1 lb extra-firm tofu, drained
¼ c nutritional yeast
1½ tsp Dijon mustard
1 tsp granulated onion powder
1 tsp granulated garlic powder
¼ tsp turmeric
salt, to taste
pepper, to taste
½ to 1 c chopped vegetables or other ingredients

1. Preheat oven to to 400°F. Grease or spray a shallow 9-inch pie dish and set aside.

2. Crumble tofu in a large bowl with your hands until it looks like feta cheese.

3. Stir in nutritional yeast, Dijon mustard, onion powder, garlic powder, turmeric, plus salt and pepper to taste until well combined.

4. Mix in vegetables or any other additional ingredients you're using.

5. Transfer mixture to pie dish and pat down firmly with a spatula until nice and tight.

6. Bake for 20 to 25 minutes, until the top is firm and slightly brown.

7. Let frittata cool for 5 minutes on the counter before serving.

8. Place a dish over top and quickly, but gently, flip frittata out.

NUTRITIONAL INFORMATION 🍜 Calories **67**; Calories from Fat **10**; Total Fat **1.1g**; Cholesterol **0mg**; Total Carbohydrate **4.9g**; Dietary Fiber **1.5g**; Sugars **1.2g**; Protein **10.3g**

Nomelet Ⓖ

Serves 2 | *Pictured opposite and on pg. 21* | Unlike other vegan omelet recipes, this nomelet is baked, freeing up your time to make home fries for brunch or get ready for work if it's a weekday.

1 12.3-oz package Mori-Nu extra-firm silken tofu
½ tsp granulated onion powder
½ tsp granulated garlic powder
¾ tsp turmeric
2 tbsp chickpea flour
2 tbsp cornstarch
¼ c non-dairy milk
2 tbsp nutritional yeast
salt, to taste
pepper, to taste

1. Preheat oven to 350°F. Grease a shallow 9-inch pie dish and set aside.
2. Blend all ingredients except salt and pepper together until smooth and creamy.
3. Add salt and pepper to taste and re-blend.
4. Divide batter in half, pouring one half into the pie dish and setting the rest aside for a later use.
5. Bake for 25 to 35 minutes or until golden and firm to the touch.
6. Let cool for 5 to 10 minutes before serving.
7. To remove omelet, place a plate over the top and flip out.
8. Remaining batter can be used to make another Nomelet. If not using immediately, store in an airtight container in the refrigerator for up to 5 days, baking as directed above.

> **CHEF'S NOTE:** *If you want to add vegetables or other toppings to your omelet, add them on top halfway through baking, but the toppings should already be cooked and prepared. Uncooked batter will keep in the fridge in an airtight container for up to 4 days.*

NUTRITIONAL INFORMATION ✎ Calories **168**; Calories from Fat **22**; Total Fat **2.4g**; Cholesterol **0mg**; Total Carbohydrate **20.4g**; Dietary Fiber **3.4g**; Sugars **3.2g**; Protein **16.8g**

Tofu Scramble

Serves 2 | *Pictured on pg. 22* | If you've never had tofu before, this is the recipe to break in your tofu shoes with. It's easy, delicious, and versatile. It's quick enough that you can make it for breakfast during the week, but I love serving it at brunch alongside French Toast (pg. 24), Breakfast Sausage Patties (pg. 140), Pancakes (pg. 28), or Corncakes (pg. 249), and fresh squeezed orange juice. Jazz up this basic recipe by adding 1 cup of chopped vegetables, mushrooms, spinach, or vegan meat.

1 lb firm or extra-firm tofu, drained
3 tbsp nutritional yeast
1 tbsp Dijon mustard
1 tsp granulated garlic powder
1 tsp granulated onion powder
½ tsp turmeric
½ tsp ground cumin
1 c vegetables, mushrooms, spinach, or vegan meat, chopped (optional)
salt, to taste
pepper, to taste

1. Place tofu in skillet and break apart with a spatula into large chunks.
2. Cook over medium-high heat until tofu releases its water, about 3 to 4 minutes.
3. Add nutritional yeast, dijon, garlic powder, onion powder, cumin and turmeric, stirring to coat evenly.
4. Break up any large remaining chunks of tofu until the tofu is crumbly and looks like scrambled eggs.
5. Continue to cook, stirring regularly, until all water has evaporated, about 10 minutes. (Add a splash of water or non-dairy milk if necessary to prevent sticking.)
6. If using, mix in vegetables, mushrooms, spinach, or vegan meat and continue to cook until everything is thoroughly warmed.
7. Add salt and pepper to taste and serve immediately.

CHEF'S NOTE: *If using vegetables, mushrooms, or spinach, line skillet with a thin layer of water and cook until desired tenderness, drain, and set aside. If using vegan meat, cook according to directions on packaging and set aside.*

NUTRITIONAL INFORMATION 🥄 Calories **121**; Calories from Fat **20**; Total Fat **2.3g**; Cholesterol **0mg**; Total Carbohydrate **7.1g**; Dietary Fiber **1.8g**; Sugars **1.8g**; Protein **18.9g**

Breakfast Burrito

Serves 4 | This is my basic breakfast burrito recipe. Feel free to add leftover cooked vegetables, Cajun Home Fries (pg. 30), black beans, fresh cilantro, Bacon Bits (pg. 137), or crumbled Spicy Sausage (pg. 150). If you're feeling fancy, serve it with a dollop of Low-Fat Guacamole (pg. 231) and Sour Cream (pg. 271).

1 recipe Tofu Scramble
  (opposite page)
4 whole-wheat wraps,
  gently heated
salsa

1. Prepare Tofu Scramble.
2. Spoon into a warmed wrap and roll up.
3. Place crease side down on the plate and generously spoon warm or room-temperature salsa over top.

VARIATIONS

Mexican Breakfast Burrito Mix in one 4-oz can of diced green chilies, Cajun Home Fries (pg. 30), and Mexican Chorizo (pg. 147).

Super Protein Breakfast Burrito Mix in one 10-oz package of frozen spinach, thawed and squeezed, with 1 cup of black beans and 1 cup of cooked quinoa or Charleston Red Rice (pg. 192).

NUTRITIONAL INFORMATION

BASIC BREAKFAST BURRITO Calories **78**; Calories from Fat **11**; Total Fat **1.2g**; Cholesterol **0mg**; Total Carbohydrate **7.6g**; Dietary Fiber **1.9g**; Sugars **2.9g**; Protein **10.5g**

MEXICAN BREAKFAST BURRITO Calories **271.4**; Calories from Fat **32.3**; Fat **2.3g**; Cholesterol **0mg**; Protein **28.5g**; Carbohydrate **33.6g**; Fiber **6.7g**; Sugar **8.5g**

SUPER PROTEIN VARIATION Calories **149**; Calories from Fat **18**; Total Fat **2.0g**; Cholesterol **0mg**; Total Carbohydrate **19.2g**; Dietary Fiber **6.5g**; Sugars **3.2g**; Protein **16.0g**

Breakfast Sandwiches

Serves 6 | *Pictured opposite* | Way better than the drive-thru, these sandwiches are healthy and delicious. They store beautifully in the fridge and reheat to perfection in a toaster oven when warmed gently for 5 to 10 minutes.

1 recipe Nomelet (pg. 17)
6 whole-wheat English
   muffins
6 vegan cheese slices
   (optional)
1 recipe Breakfast
   Sausage Patties (pg. 140)
   or vegan bacon

1. Cut out six equal slices of the Nomelet for the sandwiches and keep in a warm place.

2. In a toaster oven, toast English muffins with cheese, if using, and prepare Breakfast Sausage Patties or vegetarian bacon as directed.

3. Assemble sandwiches and serve.

NUTRITIONAL INFORMATION 🐟 Calories **104.6**; Calories from Fat **14**; Total Fat **1.5g**; Cholesterol **0mg**; Total Carbohydrate **12.5g**; Dietary Fiber **2.2g**; Sugars **1.9g**; Protein **10.3g**

No-Huevos Rancheros

Serves 4 | *Pictured opposite* | Huevos rancheros, which translates to "ranch eggs"—or more eloquently, "eggs ranch-style"—is a traditional Mexican dish served at *almuerzo* (a midmorning breakfast). I like to eat this vegan version at brunch, particularly when I'm nursing a hangover.

1 recipe Cajun Home Fries
(pg. 30)
1 recipe Tofu Scramble
(pg. 18)
1 red bell pepper, seeded
and diced
1 green bell pepper, seeded
and diced
4 to 8 whole-wheat or corn
tortillas
1 15-oz can vegetarian
refried beans
1 c salsa
1 recipe Low-Fat
Guacamole (pg. 231;
optional)
1 recipe Sour Cream
(pg. 271; optional)

1. Prepare Cajun Home Fries.

2. While fries are baking, prepare Tofu Scramble with bell peppers.

3. Once everything is cooked, place one to two tortillas on each plate and microwave 15 seconds or until very soft.

4. Spoon Tofu Scramble on one side and Cajun Home Fries on the other. Add a dollop of refried beans, salsa, and Low-Fat Guacamole or Sour Cream.

VARIATIONS

No-Huevos Divorciados Spoon plain Tofu Scramble on each side of the tortilla, leaving room in the center. Create a wall between the Tofu Scramble using refried beans or Cajun Home Fries. Place a dollop of salsa over one side and a dollop salsa verde over the other.

No-Huevos Motuleños Mix Tofu Scramble with 1 cup of cooked or canned black beans and ½ cup of cooked peas and serve over warmed tortillas with a dollop of salsa picante and a side of sliced bananas.

NUTRITIONAL INFORMATION

NO-HUEVOS RANCHEROS Calories **243**; Calories from Fat **16**; Total Fat **1.8g**; Total Carbohydrate **39g**; Dietary Fiber **11.1g**; Sugars **7.85g**; Protein **20.1g**

NO-HUEVOS DIVORCIADOS Calories **137**; Calories from Fat **18**; Total Fat **2.0g**; Cholesterol **5mg**; Total Carbohydrate **17.4g**; Dietary Fiber **5.2g**; Sugars **3.0g**; Protein **13.9g**

NO-HUEVOS MOTULEÑOS Calories **191**; Calories from Fat **18**; Total Fat **2.0g**; Cholesterol **0mg**; Total Carbohydrate **30.7g**; Dietary Fiber **6.8g**; Sugars **10.1g**; Protein **15.1g**

French Toast

Serves 4 | Right after we started dating, my boyfriend (now husband) surprised me with homemade French toast for breakfast. I knew right then he was a keeper. After we were married and vegan, my husband created this recipe so he could still make me French toast on the weekends. Serve it with Tofu Scramble (pg. 18), Breakfast Sausage Patties (pg. 140), and fresh strawberries or bananas.

8 slices whole-wheat bread
1 c non-dairy milk
¼ c chickpea flour
1 tsp ground cinnamon
1 tsp pure maple syrup
½ tsp fine salt
¼ tsp ground nutmeg
¼ tsp vanilla extract
    (optional)
extra maple syrup for
    serving

1. Cut bread in half diagonally while skillet heats.
2. Whisk non-dairy milk, flour, cinnamon, maple syrup, salt, nutmeg, and vanilla extract, if using, in a shallow bowl.
3. Spray skillet with cooking spray.
4. Dip a few slices into the mixture and transfer to the skillet.
5. Cook for 3 minutes, flip over, and cook for 3 minutes more.
6. Re-spray the skillet and repeat with remaining slices.
7. Garnish with cinnamon, confectioners' sugar, and sliced fresh fruit.

VARIATION

Gingerbread French Toast 🌸 Ⓢ 😊 ✿ 🍃 Add 1 tsp ground ginger, ¼ tsp ground cloves, and another ¼ tsp nutmeg to the non-dairy milk mixture.

NUTRITIONAL INFORMATION (4 PIECES PER SERVING)

FRENCH TOAST 🍃 Calories **70**; Calories from Fat **12**; Total Fat **1.3g**; Cholesterol **0mg**; Total Carbohydrate **11.2g**; Dietary Fiber **2.8g**; Sugars **3.9g**; Protein **3.9g**

GINGERBREAD FRENCH TOAST 🍃 Calories **73**; Calories from Fat **13**; Total Fat **1.4g**; Cholesterol **0mg**; Total Carbohydrate **11.7g**; Dietary Fiber **2.8g**; Sugars **3.9g**; Protein **4g**

Eggnog French Toast

Serves 4 | A holiday variation on French Toast! Commercial vegan eggnog may be used in place of the vanilla non-dairy milk, but omit the nutmeg and cloves.

8 slices whole-wheat bread
1 c vanilla non-dairy milk
¼ tsp ground nutmeg or mace
⅛ tsp ground cloves
¼ c chickpea flour
1 tsp pure maple syrup
½ tsp fine salt
¼ tsp pumpkin pie spice

1. Cut bread in half diagonally while skillet heats.
2. Whisk non-dairy milk with nutmeg or mace and cloves in a shallow bowl.
3. Whisk in flour, cinnamon, maple syrup, salt, and pumpkin pie spice.
4. Spray skillet with cooking spray.
5. Dip a few slices into the mixture and transfer to the skillet.
6. Cook for 3 minutes, flip over, and cook for 3 minutes more.
7. Re-spray and repeat with remaining slices.
8. Garnish with a light dash of nutmeg, confectioners' sugar, and sliced fresh bananas.

NUTRITIONAL INFORMATION (4 PIECES PER SERVING) Calories **186**; Calories from Fat **23**; Total Fat **2.5g**; Cholesterol **0mg**; Total Carbohydrate **33.4g**; Dietary Fiber **4.8g**; Sugars **3.1g**; Protein **8.2g**

Cinnamon-Banana Toast Crunch

Serves 1 | *Pictured opposite* | As a girl who grew up on frozen waffles, I still crave the ease of a frozen waffle and the sweet taste of maple syrup at breakfast. This recipe fits the bill perfectly and is my go-to breakfast any time I want French toast or waffles for breakfast but don't have the time to make them.

2 slices whole-wheat bread
¼ c pure maple syrup
1 tsp ground cinnamon
¼ tsp vanilla or banana extract (optional)
1 banana, sliced

1. Lightly toast bread.

2. While it's toasting, whisk syrup, cinnamon, and extract together. It takes a little elbow grease and a lot of whisking to fully incorporate, so keep at it.

3. Plate toast, smear syrup mixture across both slices of toast, and let it soak in, about 30 seconds to 1 minute.

4. Top each slice with fresh banana slices and garnish with a light drizzle of pure maple syrup or agave nectar, if desired.

NUTRITIONAL INFORMATION 🍽 Calories **319**; Calories from Fat **5**; Total Fat **0.6g**; Cholesterol **0mg**; Total Carbohydrate **81.8g**; Dietary Fiber **4.3g**; Sugars **61.5g**; Protein **1.4g**

Pancakes

Serves 8 | *Pictured on pg. 227 (with Blueberry Sauce)* | This is my easy pancake recipe. The batter pours beautifully, so you always end up with perfectly shaped pancakes. They're thin, much like silver dollar pancakes, but still fluffy. I like to add fresh banana slices or frozen blueberries to the batter.

1 c whole-wheat pastry
   flour
1 tbsp baking powder
½ tsp ground cinnamon
⅛ tsp fine salt
1 c non-dairy milk
2 tbsp pure maple syrup
1 tbsp raw sugar (optional)

1. Whisk flour, baking powder, cinnamon, and salt together in a large bowl.
2. Combine non-dairy milk with maple and sugar, if using.
3. Pour wet mixture into the dry mixture and stir until just combined; a few lumps are okay.
4. Let rest for 10 minutes.
5. Meanwhile, heat skillet over very low heat.
6. Transfer mixture to a large glass/liquid measuring cup or use greased ¼-cup measuring cup.
7. Spray skillet with cooking spray and pour in ¼ cup batter.
8. Cook on one side until bubbles form, gently flip, and cook for another 2 to 3 minutes.

VARIATION

Eggnog Pancakes Substitute 1 cup of vegan eggnog or 1 cup of vanilla non-dairy milk combined with ¼ tsp of nutmeg and ⅛ tsp of cloves in place of plain non-dairy milk.

NUTRITIONAL INFORMATION

PANCAKES Calories **79**; Calories from Fat **5**; Total Fat **0.5g**; Cholesterol **0mg**; Total Carbohydrate **16.3g**; Dietary Fiber **1.7g**; Sugars **3.7g**; Protein **2.3g**

EGGNOG PANCAKES Calories **79.9**; Calories from Fat **2.8**; Fat **0.3g**; Cholesterol **0mg**; Protein **2.3g**; Carbohydrate **17g**; Fiber **2.2g**; Sugar **1.3g**

Brown Rice Pancakes

Serves 8 | Brown rice flour adds a bit of a crunch and a nice nutty taste to traditional pancakes.

½ c whole-wheat pastry
　flour
½ c brown rice flour
1 tbsp baking powder
½ tsp ground cinnamon
⅛ tsp fine salt
1 c non-dairy milk
2 tbsp pure maple syrup
1 tbsp raw sugar (optional)

1. Whisk flours, baking powder, cinnamon, and salt together in a large bowl.

2. Combine non-dairy milk with maple and sugar, if using.

3. Pour wet mixture into dry and stir until just combined; a few lumps are okay.

4. Let rest for 10 minutes.

5. Meanwhile, heat skillet over very low heat.

6. Transfer mixture to a large glass/liquid measuring cup or use greased ¼-cup measuring cup.

7. Spray skillet with cooking spray and pour in ¼ cup batter.

8. Cook on one side until bubbles form, then gently flip and cook for another 2 to 3 minutes.

NUTRITIONAL INFORMATION ✎ Calories **86.4**; Calories from Fat **3.8**; Total Fat **0.4g**; Cholesterol **0mg**; Total Carbohydrate **18.5g**; Protein **2.2g**

Cajun Home Fries

Serves 4 | Pictured on pg. 22 (with No-Huevos Rancheros) | These spicy home fries are ridiculously addictive. You'll be popping them in your mouth while plating other food and "accidentally" leaving a few on the tray in the kitchen so you can go back for more in secret.

2 medium russet potatoes, diced
about 2 tsp granulated garlic powder
about 2 tsp granulated onion powder
about 1 tsp onion flakes
about ¼ tsp paprika
cayenne powder, to taste
salt, to taste
pepper, to taste

1. Preheat oven to 400°F. Grease cookie sheet and set aside.
2. Place potatoes in a mixing bowl.
3. Spray with cooking spray and sprinkle spices over top. Be generous with garlic and onion, but do not use too much cayenne or paprika. Add salt and pepper.
4. Mix to evenly coat. Re-spray and repeat.
5. Transfer to cookie sheet, making sure there is no overlap.
6. Bake for 15 to 25 minutes, or until fully cooked and crisp.

Herbed Home Fries

Serves 4 | Pictured opposite | These add a great contrast to brunch foods like Tofu Scramble (pg. 18), but they're also a great mashed-potato alternative.

2 medium russet potatoes, diced
about 2 tsp granulated garlic powder
about 2 tsp granulated onion powder
about 1 tsp Italian seasoning
salt, to taste

1. Preheat oven to 400°F. Grease cookie sheet and set aside.
2. Place potatoes in a mixing bowl.
3. Spray with cooking spray and sprinkle spices over top. Be generous with garlic and onion. Add salt.
4. Mix to evenly coat. Re-spray and repeat.
5. Transfer to cookie sheet, making sure there is no overlap.
6. Bake for 15 to 25 minutes, or until fully cooked and crisp.

NUTRITIONAL INFORMATION

CAJUN HOME FRIES ⬲ Calories **87**; Calories from Fat **2**; Total Fat **0.2g**; Cholesterol **0mg**; Total Carbohydrate **19.7g**; Dietary Fiber **3.0g**; Sugars **2.3g**; Protein **2.3g**

HERBED HOME FRIES ⬲ Calories **86**; Calories from Fat **4**; Total Fat **0.5g**; Cholesterol **1mg**; Total Carbohydrate **18.8g**; Dietary Fiber **2.8g**; Sugars **2.1g**; Protein **2.2g**

Sweet Potato Home Fries

Serves 4 | *Pictured opposite* | Sometimes you need to shake things up a bit and use sweet potatoes. The inclusion of apple makes these home fries naturally sweet and extra delicious.

about ¾ tsp dried rosemary
2 medium sweet potatoes, diced
1 small cooking apple, cored and diced
salt, to taste
pepper, to taste

1. Preheat oven to 400°F. Grease cookie sheet and set aside.

2. Grind rosemary with a mortar and pestle until it reaches the consistency of sea salt, but not so finely that it's like a powder.

3. Place potatoes and apples in a mixing bowl.

4. Spray with cooking spray and sprinkle rosemary plus salt and pepper over top.

5. Mix to evenly coat. Re-spray and repeat.

6. Repeat mixing for a third time if necessary.

7. Transfer to cookie sheet, making sure there is no overlap.

8. Bake for 15 to 25 minutes, or until fully cooked and crisp.

NUTRITIONAL INFORMATION 🥄 Calories **70**; Calories from Fat **1**; Total Fat **0.1g**; Cholesterol **0mg**; Total Carbohydrate **16.9g**; Dietary Fiber **2.7g**; Sugars **5.5g**; Protein **1.1g**

Muffins & Breads

Cinnamon Buns

Serves 6 | *Pictured opposite* | I love cinnamon buns. There is something bewitching about sugar and cinnamon gooeyness that I can't deny! One weekend I dared to wonder if I could make vegan cinnamon buns that were whole-wheat and fat-free. Turns out I can. Dare to dream, my friends, dare to dream.

¾ c non-dairy milk
2¼ tsp active yeast
3 c whole-wheat pastry flour
1 tbsp baking powder
¼ c raw sugar
2 tsp ground cinnamon, divided
¼ tsp fine salt
5 tbsp unsweetened applesauce
4 tbsp brown sugar
2 tbsp raisins (optional)
1 c confectioners' sugar
1 tsp non-dairy milk

1. Preheat oven to 350°F. Grease or spray a round 8-inch cake pan and set aside.

2. Gently warm non-dairy milk to approximately 110°F. Sprinkle yeast in and let it dissolve, about 5 minutes.

3. Meanwhile, whisk 2 cups of flour in a mixing bowl with baking powder, sugar, 1 tsp cinnamon, and salt.

4. Stir in applesauce and non-dairy milk mixture, using a spatula to combine, then stir in ½ cup of flour.

5. Stir in remaining flour and knead in the mixing bowl 15 to 20 times until elastic and not excessively sticky.

6. Flour a rolling pin and roll dough out into a large, thin rectangle.

7. In a small bowl, combine brown sugar, raisins, if using, and remaining cinnamon. Spoon and spread this mix around the center of the dough, leaving 1-inch edge clear.

8. Gently but tightly roll the dough up. Using a string, pizza cutter or sharp knife, cut roll into six equal pieces.

9. Place buns in the prepared pan; a tight fit is okay.

10. Bake for 25 minutes, until slightly golden and thoroughly cooked.

11. While baking, prepare icing by mixing confectioners' sugar with non-dairy milk until a thin glaze forms.

12. Drizzle icing over the buns while they're still warm.

NUTRITIONAL INFORMATION 🥄 Calories **385**; Calories from Fat **12**; Total Fat **1.4g**; Cholesterol **0mg**; Total Carbohydrate **85.4g**; Dietary Fiber **7.2g**; Sugars **37.6g**; Protein **7.5g**

Biscuits

Serves 6 | These biscuits are a bit dry when eaten by themselves, but the slight dryness makes them perfect for sopping up liquid. Dunk them, drown them in gravy, clean the bottom of your soup bowl with them ... you get the picture.

1 c whole-wheat pastry flour
2 tsp baking powder
½ tsp baking soda
¼ tsp fine salt
½ banana, cold (do not slice!)
⅓ c non-dairy milk

1. Preheat oven to 425°F.
2. Combine flour, baking powder, baking soda, and salt in food processor and pulse a few times to ensure even distribution.
3. Add banana and let motor run until pebbles form.
4. Transfer to a bowl and stir in non-dairy milk. It may take a while to incorporate, but that's okay. It might also seem too wet, but it's not.
5. Drop spoonfuls onto a greased cookie sheet and bake for 5 to 10 minutes, until golden and slightly brown at the edges.

> **CHEF'S NOTE:** *To avoid a hint of banana flavor use a barely ripe or still slightly green banana.*

NUTRITIONAL INFORMATION 🍴 Calories **88**; Calories from Fat **4**; Total Fat **0.5g**; Cholesterol **0mg**; Total Carbohydrate **18.1g**; Dietary Fiber **2.4g**; Sugars **1.5g**; Protein **2.4g**

Maple-Cornbread Biscuits

Serves 6 | I love cornbread and I love biscuits. This is a happy marriage between the two, with a nice, sweet addition of maple syrup. Eat them for breakfast or alongside a big bowl of Chili sans Carne (pg. 81).

½ c whole-wheat pastry
  flour
⅓ c cornmeal
2 tsp baking powder
½ tsp baking soda
¼ tsp fine salt
½ banana, cold (do not
  slice!)
¼ c non-dairy milk
2 tbsp pure maple syrup

1. Preheat oven to 425°F.

2. Combine flour, cornmeal, baking powder, baking soda, and salt in food processor and pulse a few times to ensure even distribution.

3. Add banana and let motor run until pebbles form.

4. Transfer to a bowl and stir in non-dairy milk and maple syrup. It may take a while to incorporate, but that's okay. It might also seem too wet, but it's not.

5. Drop spoonfuls onto a greased cookie sheet and bake for 5 to 10 minutes, until golden and slightly brown at the edges.

> **CHEF'S NOTE:** *For a stronger maple flavor, add a few drops of maple extract.*

NUTRITIONAL INFORMATION ✐ Calories **104**; Calories from Fat **6**; Total Fat **0.7g**; Cholesterol **0mg**; Total Carbohydrate **23.0g**; Dietary Fiber **2.1g**; Sugars **5.5g**; Protein **2.2g**

Apple Crisp Muffins

Serves 12 | *Pictured opposite* | As the name suggests, these muffins embody all the best qualities of an apple crisp. They have just the right balance between apple, cinnamon, brown sugar, and oats but come in a nicely wrapped edible package. I like to make these with McIntosh apples when they're in season, but most apples can be substituted. I also like to leave the skin on the apples for added nutrients, but you can peel them if you prefer.

1½ c whole-wheat pastry flour
½ c rolled oats
2 tsp baking powder
1 tsp baking soda
¼ tsp fine salt
2 tsp ground cinnamon
few dashes of ground nutmeg
few dashes of ground ginger
1 c unsweetened applesauce
½ c raw sugar
¼ c brown sugar
¼ c pure maple syrup
1 c chopped apples

1. Preheat oven 350°F. Grease or spray a muffin tin or paper liners, if using.

2. In a large bowl, whisk flour, oats, baking powder, baking soda, salt, and spices together until well combined.

3. Add applesauce, sugars, and maple syrup, then stir until almost combined.

4. Add apple pieces, stirring until just combined.

5. Spoon into muffin cups ¾ full.

6. Sprinkle additional oats and brown sugar on top, if desired.

7. Bake for 18 to 25 minutes, or until a toothpick inserted in the center comes out clean.

8. Transfer to a wire cooling rack.

NUTRITIONAL INFORMATION ⌇ Calories **124**; Calories from Fat **3**; Total Fat **0.4g**; Cholesterol **0mg**; Total Carbohydrate **28.8g**; Dietary Fiber **2.4g**; Sugars **15.4g**; Protein **1.8g**

Blueberry Oatmeal Muffins

Serves 12 | I love blueberry oatmeal but hate that it's not easily portable. Now it is with these healthy muffins! Don't be shy with the ground ginger; it gives these muffins a nice zing.

1½ c whole-wheat pastry flour
½ c rolled oats
2 tsp baking powder
1 tsp baking soda
¼ tsp fine salt
1 tsp ground cinnamon
½ tsp ground ginger, or to taste
1 c unsweetened applesauce
½ c brown sugar
¼ c pure maple syrup
¾ c frozen wild blueberries

1. Preheat oven 350°F. Grease or spray a muffin tin or paper liners, if using.

2. In a large bowl, whisk flour, oats, baking powder, baking soda, salt, and spices together until well combined.

3. Add applesauce, sugar, and maple syrup and stir until almost combined.

4. Add blueberries, stirring until just combined.

5. Spoon into muffin cups ¾ full.

6. Sprinkle additional oats and brown sugar on top if desired.

7. Bake for 18 to 25 minutes, or until a toothpick inserted in the center comes out clean.

8. Transfer to a wire cooling rack.

NUTRITIONAL INFORMATION Calories **123**; Calories from Fat **5**; Total Fat **0.5g**; Cholesterol **0mg**; Total Carbohydrate **27.8g**; Dietary Fiber **2.4g**; Sugars **12.7g**; Protein **2.1g**

Spiced Carrot Muffins Ⓕ Ⓢ ✪

Serves 12 | *Pictured on pg. 34* | These muffins are the slightly healthier and sassy sister to my beloved Carrot Cake Cupcakes (pg. 213). They're perfect for breakfast but also make a great mid-afternoon snack.

1½ c whole-wheat pastry flour
1 tsp baking soda
2 tsp baking powder
½ tsp fine salt
½ tsp ground cinnamon
¼ tsp ground cloves, or more to taste
¼ tsp ground nutmeg
½ tsp allspice (optional)
½ c raw sugar
1½ c unsweetened applesauce
1 tsp vanilla extract
1 large carrot, shredded

1. Preheat oven to 350°F. Grease or spray a muffin tin or paper liners, if using.

2. In a large bowl, whisk flour, baking soda, baking powder, salt, and spices together.

3. Add sugar, applesauce, vanilla, and carrots to the middle of the mixture, stirring until just combined.

4. The mixture may appear too dry initially, but it's not; keep mixing.

5. Spoon each muffin cup ¾ full and bake for 18 to 25 minutes, or until a toothpick inserted in the center comes out clean.

6. Transfer to a wire cooling rack.

VARIATION

Carrot-Raisin Muffins Ⓕ Ⓢ 😊 ⟿ Reduce sugar to ¼ cup, omit cloves and allspice, and add ¼ to ½ cup of raisins that were soaked in cool water overnight or in hot water for at least 10 minutes.

NUTRITIONAL INFORMATION (PER MUFFIN)

SPICED CARROT MUFFINS ⟿ Calories **110**; Calories from Fat **3**; Total Fat **0.3g**; Cholesterol **0mg**; Total Carbohydrate **24.9g**; Dietary Fiber **2.5g**; Sugars **12.3g**; Protein **1.7g**

CARROT-RAISIN MUFFINS ⟿ Calories **102**; Calories from Fat **3**; Total Fat **0.3g**; Cholesterol **0mg**; Total Carbohydrate **23.1g**; Dietary Fiber **2.6g**; Sugars **10.0g**; Protein **1.8g**

Chocolate-Zucchini Muffins

Serves 12 | *Pictured opposite* | I know what you're thinking: "Those two foods don't go together." But they do! The inclusion of zucchini makes these muffins ultra-moist and wholesome. The zucchini bits also all but vanish during the baking process, making them completely undetectable. Go on and fool your kids, friends, and co-workers with these healthy chocolate darlings!

1¼ c whole-wheat pastry flour
¼ c unsweetened cocoa
1¼ tsp baking powder
¾ tsp baking soda
½ tsp fine salt
1 tsp ground cinnamon
1 ripe banana, mashed
½ c unsweetened applesauce
½ to 1 c raw sugar
¼ c non-dairy milk
1 tsp vanilla extract
1 c shredded zucchini
¼ c vegan chocolate chips (optional)

1. Preheat oven to 350°F. Grease or spray a muffin tin or paper liners, if using.

2. In a medium bowl, whisk flour, cocoa, baking powder, baking soda, salt, and cinnamon together.

3. In a large bowl, cream mashed banana with applesauce and sugar then add non-dairy milk, vanilla, zucchini, and chips, if using, stirring to combine.

4. Add the dry mixture into the wet mixture in 3 to 4 batches, stirring until just combined.

5. Spoon into muffin cups ¾ full.

6. Bake for 18 to 25 minutes, or until a toothpick inserted in the center comes out clean.

7. Transfer to a wire cooling rack.

CHEF'S NOTE: *Use the reduced amount of sugar for a less sweet muffin and all the sugar for a more dessert-like treat.*

NUTRITIONAL INFORMATION 🥄 Calories **150**; Calories from Fat **7**; Total Fat **0.8g**; Cholesterol **0mg**; Total Carbohydrate **34.2g**; Dietary Fiber **3.7g**; Sugars **16.4g**; Protein **3.0g**

Maple Muffins Ⓕ Ⓢ 😀 ✪

Serves 12 | These are my favorite muffins. They're kissed with pure maple syrup and use up leftover sweet potatoes or pumpkin puree. I like to serve them for breakfast on Thanksgiving morning and at brunch on New Year's Day.

1½ c whole-wheat pastry flour
2 tsp baking powder
1 tsp baking soda
2 tsp pumpkin pie spice
pinch of fine salt
1 c pure pumpkin or sweet potato puree
1 c unsweetened applesauce
¾ c brown sugar
¼ c pure maple syrup

1. Preheat oven to 350°F. Grease or spray a muffin tin or paper liners, if using.

2. In a large bowl, whisk flour, baking powder, baking soda, pumpkin pie spice, and salt until well combined.

3. Add pumpkin or sweet potato puree, applesauce, sugar, and maple syrup, then stir until just combined.

4. Spoon mixture into muffin cups ¾ full.

5. Bake for 18 to 25 minutes, or until a toothpick inserted in the center comes out clean.

6. Transfer to a wire cooling rack.

NUTRITIONAL INFORMATION 🥄 Calories **102**; Calories from Fat **3**; Total Fat **0.3g**; Cholesterol **0mg**; Total Carbohydrate **23.1g**; Dietary Fiber **2.6g**; Sugars **10.0g**; Protein **1.8g**

Banana Bread Ⓕ Ⓢ 😀 ✪

Makes 12 slices (12 servings) | I don't like to throw words such as "awesome" around too lightly, but this banana bread is awesome! It's so delicious and moist you'll never believe it's made with whole wheat and has zero added fat!

¼ c non-dairy milk
¼ tsp lemon juice
4 or 5 spotted or browning bananas
½ c dark brown sugar
½ c raw sugar
1 tsp ground cinnamon
½ tsp ground nutmeg
2 c whole-wheat flour
1 tsp baking soda
½ tsp baking powder
1 tsp vanilla extract
2 tbsp pure maple syrup

1. Preheat oven to 350°F. Grease or spray a standard 8-inch loaf pan and set aside.

2. Whisk the non-dairy milk and lemon juice together until bubbly and set aside.

3. Cream bananas with sugars by hand using a spatula or in a food processor until smooth and creamy; set aside.

4. In a large bowl, whisk spices, flour, baking soda, and baking powder together.

5. Add milk–lemon juice and banana mixture, as well as all remaining ingredients, to the flour mixture and stir until just combined.

6. Pour into loaf pan, using a spatula to evenly distribute and smooth out the top.

7. Make a tent over the pan with a large piece of aluminum foil.

8. Bake for 45 minutes to 1 hour, or until a toothpick inserted in the center comes out clean.

VARIATION

Super Awesome Banana Bread Ⓕ Ⓢ 😀 ✪ ✎ Adding ¼ tsp of almond extract plus 1 tsp of cherry extract takes this bread to a whole new level of awesomeness.

NUTRITIONAL INFORMATION ✎ Calories **178**; Calories from Fat 4; Total Fat **0.4g**; Cholesterol **0mg**; Total Carbohydrate **41.9g**; Dietary Fiber **1.7g**; Sugars **21.2g**; Protein **2.7g**

Cornbread

Serves 6 | *Pictured opposite* | This is my favorite cornbread recipe. It's quick and simple—the kind of recipe you can whip up at any time because you always have the ingredients on hand. It's also a complementary side dish to almost every meal and makes a great breakfast or snack.

1 c cornmeal
1 c whole-wheat pastry
   flour
1 tbsp baking powder
½ tsp fine salt
1 c non-dairy milk
¼ c unsweetened
   applesauce
¼ c pure maple syrup
2 tbsp raw sugar (optional)

1. Preheat oven to 400°F.
2. Whisk cornmeal, flour, baking powder, and salt together in a large bowl.
3. Add non-dairy milk, applesauce, maple syrup, and sugar, if using, on top.
4. Using a spatula, stir until just combined.
5. Pour batter into a greased or nonstick shallow 9-inch pie dish, cast iron skillet, or a square casserole dish.
6. Bake for approximately 20 minutes or until a toothpick inserted in the center comes out clean.

VARIATION

Lemony Cornbread 🄢 😊 🍃 Mix in the zest of 1 lemon before baking.

> CHEF'S NOTE: *For a more dense and corn-flavored bread, use 1½ cups of cornmeal and ½ cup of flour. You can also add ½ cup of frozen corn kernels if you prefer.*

NUTRITIONAL INFORMATION 🍃 Calories **200**; Calories from Fat **13**; Total Fat **1.4g**; Cholesterol **0mg**; Total Carbohydrate **42.8g**; Dietary Fiber **3.8g**; Sugars **10.0g**; Protein **4.7g**

Gingerbread Mini-Loaves

Each loaf serves 6; makes 2 mini-loaves | *Pictured opposite* | I miss the days when neighbors got together for potlucks and people gave baked goods as gifts during the holiday season. I'm trying to bring all that back with these mini-loaves. If you find one under your tree without a card, it's from me.

2 c whole-wheat pastry flour
2 tsp baking powder
½ tsp baking soda
4 tsp ground ginger
2 tsp ground cinnamon
1 tsp allspice
½ tsp ground cloves
¼ tsp fine salt
¾ c brown sugar
¾ c canned pure pumpkin
¼ c molasses
2 tbsp crystallized ginger, finely chopped (optional)

1. Preheat oven to 350°F.
2. Whisk flour, baking powder, baking soda, spices, and salt together in a large bowl and set aside.
3. In a medium bowl, combine sugar, pumpkin, and molasses.
4. Pour wet mixture into dry mixture and add ½ cup of water.
5. Stroke about 10 times, add chopped ginger and ¼ cup of water, then stir until incorporated. Be careful not to overmix.
6. Transfer batter to two nonstick mini-loaf pans, filling each ¾ full. Bake for 40 to 45 minutes or until a toothpick inserted in the center comes out clean and the loaves have peaked.

CHEF'S NOTE: *In a pinch, applesauce may be substituted for the pure pumpkin, but pumpkin is preferred.*

NUTRITIONAL INFORMATION Calories **137**; Calories from Fat **4**; Total Fat **0.5g**; Cholesterol **0mg**; Total Carbohydrate **31.2g**; Dietary Fiber **2.8g**; Sugars **13.1g**; Protein **2.3g**

Pumpkin Bread Ⓕ Ⓢ ✪

Makes 12 slices (12 servings) | *Pictured opposite* | If you love banana bread you're in for a real treat with this fall favorite. A slice goes perfectly with a cup of warm apple cider for breakfast, or treat yourself to some for dessert if you opt for the frosting.

¼ c non-dairy milk
¼ tsp lemon juice
1 15-oz can pure pumpkin
1 c brown sugar
2 tbsp pure maple syrup
1 tsp vanilla extract
2 tbsp pumpkin pie spice
2 c whole-wheat flour
1 tsp baking soda
½ tsp baking powder
Maple Icing (pg. 223; optional)

CHEF'S NOTE:
If you're not using icing, pepitas (hulled pumpkin seeds) make a lovely garnish. Sprinkle over top before baking.

1. Preheat oven to 350°F. Grease or spray a standard 8-inch loaf pan.
2. Whisk non-dairy milk and lemon juice together until bubbly and set aside.
3. In a medium mixing bowl, cream pumpkin, sugar, maple syrup, and vanilla together.
4. In a large bowl, whisk pumpkin pie spice, flour, baking soda, and baking powder together.
5. Pour wet mixture into dry mixture and stir until just combined.
6. Pour into loaf pan, using a spatula to evenly distribute and smooth out the top.
7. Make a tent over the pan with a large piece of aluminum foil.
8. Bake for 1 hour, or until a toothpick inserted in the center comes out clean.
9. Once the bread has cooled but is still slightly warm, gently remove it from the pan and onto a serving plate.
10. Slather icing over top, allowing it to run down the sides. Then let the bread cool and icing firm into a glaze.

NUTRITIONAL INFORMATION (WITHOUT ICING) 🥄 Calories **148**; Calories from Fat **4**; Total Fat **0.5g**; Cholesterol **0mg**; Total Carbohydrate **33.8g**; Dietary Fiber **1.8g**; Sugars **15.2g**; Protein **2.7g**

Scones

Serves 12 | *Raisin Scones variation pictured opposite* | I'm not sure if it's their cute figures or the way scones remind you of a muffin and a biscuit, but something about scones is magical. I've wanted to make fat-free scones for a while now but couldn't come up with a way to replace all that butter. Then it hit me—a cold banana!

1¼ c non-dairy milk
2 tsp lemon juice
3 c whole-wheat pastry
    flour
2 tbsp baking powder
pinch of fine salt
⅓ c raw sugar (optional)
1 cold banana, peeled and
    cut in half

1. Preheat oven to 350°F. Grease a cookie sheet or line with parchment paper.

2. Whisk non-dairy milk and lemon juice together, then set aside to curdle.

3. Combine flour, baking powder, salt, and sugar, if using, together in food processor and pulse a few times to ensure even distribution of the ingredients.

4. Add banana and let motor run until it has been incorporated and the flour has little pebbles of banana.

5. Transfer to a mixing bowl and pour in non-dairy milk and optional ingredients (see variations), stirring until just combined.

6. Using a wide ¼ c measuring cup, scoop up batter and drop onto prepared cookie sheet.

7. Bake for 15 to 20 minutes, or until firm to the touch.

NUTRITIONAL INFORMATION

BASIC SCONES ⤳ Calories **129**; Calories from Fat **7**; Total Fat **0.8g**; Cholesterol **0mg**; Total Carbohydrate **26.3g**; Dietary Fiber **3.4g**; Sugars **1.9g**; Protein **3.7g**

BLUEBERRY SCONES ⤳ Calories **136**; Calories from Fat **7**; Total Fat **0.8g**; Cholesterol **0mg**; Total Carbohydrate **28.1g**; Dietary Fiber **3.7g**; Sugars **3.0g**; Protein **3.8g**

CHOCOLATE CHIP SCONES ⤳ Calories **142**; Calories from Fat **13**; Total Fat **1.4g**; Cholesterol **0mg**; Total Carbohydrate **28.0g**; Dietary Fiber **3.6g**; Sugars **3.4g**; Protein **3.9g**

ROSEMARY SCONES ⤳ Calories **133**; Calories from Fat **8**; Total Fat **0.9g**; Cholesterol **0mg**; Total Carbohydrate **27.1g**; Dietary Fiber **3.9g**; Sugars **1.9g**; Protein **3.8g**

RAISIN SCONES ⤳ Calories **148**; Calories from Fat **8**; Total Fat **0.8g**; Cholesterol **0mg**; Total Carbohydrate **31.4g**; Dietary Fiber **3.7g**; Sugars **5.5g**; Protein **4.0g**

CHEF'S NOTE: *For best results, use a barely ripe banana that is still slightly green at the ends and has been chilled for at least 15 minutes. The firmness of the banana works the way cold butter or shortening does. The banana must be very firm in order to be cut in rather than mixed in. A very ripe or otherwise soft and mushy banana will break down into the mixture, rather than creating the pebbles. It's also very important that you only cut the banana in half and not in slices. Do not use previously frozen bananas, even if thawed.*

VARIATIONS

Blueberry Scones ⬤ Ⓕ Ⓢ ☺ ∽ Add 1 c of frozen wild blueberries and a few dashes of ground ginger.

Chocolate Chip Scones ⬤ Ⓢ ☺ ✪ ∽ Add ½ c of vegan chocolate chips with a few dashes of ground cinnamon.

Rosemary Scones ⬤ Ⓕ Ⓢ ∽ Add ¼ c of fresh rosemary, chopped.

Raisin Scones ⬤ Ⓕ Ⓢ ∽ Add 1 c of raisins with 1 tbsp of pumpkin pie spice or 2 tsp of cinnamon.

Soups, Dals, & Chilis

Comforting Winter Soup

Serves 4 | If you find yourself feeling under the weather during the winter, warm up with a bowl of this seasonal, comforting soup. Serve with toast, Biscuits (pg. 38), or Cornbread (pg. 49).

1 small bunch kale
4 c vegetable broth, divided
1 medium onion, diced
4 garlic cloves, minced
2 celery stalks, sliced
2 large carrots, peeled
   and sliced
1 leek, white parts only,
   thinly sliced
1 tbsp Italian seasoning
   or Poultry Seasoning
   Mix (pg. 273)
2 bay leaves
1 tbsp mild curry powder
¼ tsp ground ginger
salt, to taste
pepper, to taste

1. Remove stems from kale and tear into bite-sized pieces and set aside.

2. Line a large pot with 2 cups of broth and add onion, garlic, celery, carrots, leek, seasoning blend, bay leaves, and curry powder.

3. Bring to a boil over high heat and continue to boil until onion is translucent, about 5 minutes.

4. Add remaining broth and reduce heat to medium.

5. Once boiling, add kale, stirring constantly until wilted, soft, and incorporated in soup, about 2 minutes.

6. Remove from heat, add ginger, then salt and pepper.

7. Remove bay leaves before serving.

NUTRITIONAL INFORMATION ✐ Calories **95**; Calories from Fat **7**; Total Fat **0.8g**; Cholesterol **0mg**; Total Carbohydrate **21.4g**; Dietary Fiber **3.6g**; Sugars **5.0g**; Protein **3.1g**

Sweet and Spicy Butternut Soup

Serves 2 | The perfect balance between sweet and spicy gives an edgy feel to traditional butternut squash soup.

1 small butternut squash,
   cooked
2 4-oz cans green chilies
½ c non-dairy milk
1 tsp pure maple syrup, or
   to taste
½ c broth or non-dairy milk
salt, to taste
hot sauce, to taste

1. Steam, bake, or microwave butternut squash. I prefer to steam the entire squash in my steamer until fork-tender, about 35 to 40 minutes.

2. Once cooked, peel away skin and discard seedy center from butternut squash.

3. Transfer butternut squash to a blender and blend with chilies, non-dairy milk, and maple syrup.

4. Add broth or more non-dairy milk as necessary to achieve a smooth and creamy texture.

5. Transfer to a saucepan, add salt, and warm over low heat. Drizzle hot sauce over top before serving.

VARIATION

Spicy Butternut Soup F G S ✎ Add cayenne powder to taste.

NUTRITIONAL INFORMATION ✎ Calories **152**; Calories from Fat **7**; Total Fat **0.7g**; Cholesterol **0mg**; Total Carbohydrate **35.8g**; Dietary Fiber **8.6g**; Sugars **8.7g**; Protein **3.8g**

Aztec Corn Soup

Serves 2 | *Pictured opposite* | This soup is a nutritional superhero, bursting with protein and important nutrients like fiber, magnesium, and vitamin C.

¼ c uncooked quinoa or
    amaranth
2 c frozen corn, thawed
1 4-oz can green chilies
1 c non-dairy milk
½ c canned black beans,
    rinsed and drained
white pepper, to taste
1 to 2 tsp pure maple syrup
hot sauce, to taste

1. Cook the quinoa or amaranth in 1 cup of water for 15 to 20 minutes or until cooked and most of the water has been absorbed.

2. Transfer to a blender and combine with 1½ cups of the corn (reserving ½ cup of corn), green chilies, and non-dairy milk.

3. Blend until smooth or to desired consistency.

4. Return to saucepan and stir in reserved corn and black beans.

5. Heat thoroughly, adding white pepper and maple syrup.

6. Garnish with drops of hot sauce and serve.

NUTRITIONAL INFORMATION ☞ Calories **319**; Calories from Fat **42**; Total Fat **4.6g**; Cholesterol **0mg**; Total Carbohydrate **60.1g**; Dietary Fiber **11.0g**; Sugars **9.9g**; Protein **14.5g**

Creamy Carrot Soup

Serves 2 | *Pictured opposite* | Oats are the magical ingredient in this soup. They give the soup a texture it wouldn't otherwise have and also impart a lot of creamy flavor without using actual cream. This soup also whips up in an instant!

1 lb carrots, peeled and
    sliced
1 small onion, diced
¼ c instant oats
½ c non-dairy milk
½ tsp ground ginger
¼ tsp allspice
salt, to taste
pepper, to taste

1. In a medium saucepan, combine 2 cups of water, carrots, onion, and oats over high heat.

2. Bring to a boil, then reduce heat to medium.

3. Continue to cook, stirring frequently, until oats are cooked and carrots are fork-tender, about 5 minutes.

4. Transfer to a blender, in batches if necessary, and combine with non-dairy milk. Blend until smooth and creamy, adding an extra splash of non-dairy milk if needed.

5. Transfer back to saucepan and stir in ginger and allspice.

6. Gently reheat and add salt and pepper.

7. Optional: Garnish with chopped scallions and fresh pepper.

NUTRITIONAL INFORMATION ⬤ Calories **147**; Calories from Fat **14**; Total Fat **1.6g**; Cholesterol **0mg**; Total Carbohydrate **31.0g**; Dietary Fiber **7.8g**; Sugars **13.8g**; Protein **4.8g**

African Kale and Yam Soup

Serves 2 | *Pictured opposite and on pg. 56* | This soup has a wonderful ethnic feel to it. The broth is especially flavorful, so be sure to have toast or Biscuits (pg. 38) on hand so you can soak up every last drop. Sweet potatoes may be substituted for yams.

1 small red onion, thinly sliced
2 c vegetable broth
2 c peeled and diced yams
5 c kale, torn into bite-sized pieces
2 tsp chili powder
1 tsp ground cumin
1 tsp granulated garlic powder
¼ tsp red pepper flakes, or to taste
1 tsp mild curry powder
1 tbsp yellow miso paste
¼ tsp cinnamon

1. Line a medium pot with ¼ cup of water and cook onion over high heat until translucent, about 3 minutes.

2. Add broth, yams, and ¾ cups of water and bring to a boil.

3. Once boiling, reduce heat to medium and cook until yams are almost fork-tender, about 3 minutes.

4. Immediately add kale and remaining ingredients. Continue to cook, stirring frequently, until kale is dark green and soft, about 3 minutes more.

5. Set aside for 5 to 10 minutes, allowing flavors to merge, then serve.

NUTRITIONAL INFORMATION 🥄 Calories **311**; Calories from Fat **25**; Total Fat **2.8g**; Cholesterol **0mg**; Total Carbohydrate **67.9g**; Dietary Fiber **11.3g**; Sugars **4.0g**; Protein **9.7g**

CHEF'S NOTE: *Spaghetti squash can be steamed, baked, or cooked in the microwave (my preferred method). Using a fork, poke holes in the squash and microwave for 10 minutes on high. Turn squash over and repeat as necessary until it is fork-tender. Allow to cool to safely handle squash, then slice open, remove seedy matter, and run fork along squash from top to bottom to form strands.*

Tomato Soup with Spaghetti Squash

Serves 6 | *Pictured opposite* | I like to call this "Spaghetti Soup" because it sort of looks like the inverse of spaghetti with marinara. Instead of a plate of spaghetti with a little sauce, you're getting a bowl of "sauce" and a few strands of "spaghetti." I also like to serve the tomato soup by itself with vegan grilled-cheese sandwiches—perfect for dunking!

1 14-oz can whole peeled
    plum tomatoes
2 c vegetable broth
1 tbsp onion flakes
a dash of granulated garlic
    powder
2 tsp Italian seasoning, or
    to taste
1 bay leaf
1 tbsp white vinegar
5 to 10 baby carrots, minced
a dash of red pepper flakes
1 tsp mild curry powder
1 to 2 tbsp raw sugar or 1
    to 2 tsp agave nectar, as
    needed
1 to 2 c cooked spaghetti
    squash
salt, to taste
pepper, to taste
vegan Parmesan (optional)

1. Carefully drain the tomato sauce from the can into a large soup pot.

2. Carefully remove each tomato and gently squeeze its liquids into the pot.

3. Pull the whole tomatoes apart into bite-sized pieces and toss in.

4. Add broth, onion flakes, garlic powder, Italian seasoning, bay leaf, vinegar, carrots, red pepper flakes, and curry powder, stirring to combine.

5. Cover and bring to a boil, then reduce heat to low and simmer for 25 minutes.

6. If the soup is too acidic, add raw sugar or agave as needed. Continue to cook for 5 more minutes.

7. Remove bay leaf and add salt and pepper.

8. Ladle soup into bowls just slightly more than halfway.

9. Add cooked spaghetti squash in the center and sprinkle vegan Parmesan over top if desired.

10. Store leftover soup and squash separately.

NUTRITIONAL INFORMATION 🥄 Calories **52**; Calories from Fat **4**; Total Fat **0.5g**; Cholesterol **0mg**; Total Carbohydrate **11.8g**; Dietary Fiber **1.8g**; Sugars **5.6g**; Protein **1.6g**

Tortilla Soup

Serves 4 | *Pictured opposite* | Tortilla soup is a California comfort food. Thickened with corn tortillas instead of cream, tortilla soup is filling but also slimming! Make sure to use low-sodium soy sauce and no-salt added or low-sodium vegetable broth in this recipe.

1 large sweet onion, diced
4 garlic cloves, minced
1 tsp chili powder
1 tsp dried marjoram or
     oregano
2 tsp ground cumin
2 c vegetable broth
1 15-oz can fire-roasted
     diced tomatoes
1 4-oz can diced green
     chilies, drained
¼ c ketchup
2 tbsp low-sodium soy sauce
2 corn tortillas, chopped
hot sauce, to taste
salt, to taste
pepper, to taste
¼ c fresh cilantro, coarsely
     chopped
Crispy Tortilla Sticks
     (pg. 239)

1. Line a medium pot with a thin layer of water.
2. Add onion, then cook over medium heat for 2 minutes. Add garlic and continue to cook until onion is translucent and most of the water has evaporated.
3. Add chili powder, marjoram or oregano, and cumin, stirring to cover the onion and garlic with the spices, then continuing to stir until all the liquid has been absorbed and the spices are fragrant, about 30 seconds.
4. Add broth, tomatoes with their juices, and chilies, stirring to combine.
5. Bring to a boil, then cover and simmer over low heat for 15 minutes.
6. Transfer half of the mixture to your blender and whiz until smooth, or use an immersion blender to slightly, but not completely, puree the soup.
7. Return to the pot, add ketchup, 1 cup of water, soy sauce, and corn tortillas.
8. Bring to a boil, cover, reduce heat to medium, and cook over medium heat until tortillas have fallen apart and thickened the soup, about 5 to 10 minutes. Use a whisk to help incorporate if necessary.
9. Add hot sauce, salt, and pepper if desired. Let soup rest 5 minutes.
10. Stir in cilantro and ladle into bowls. Top with Crispy Tortilla Sticks and serve.

NUTRITIONAL INFORMATION ✎ Calories **157**; Calories from Fat **15**; Total Fat **1.7g**; Cholesterol **0mg**; Total Carbohydrate **33.5g**; Dietary Fiber **5.7g**; Sugars **8.9g**; Protein **4.7g**

Curried Sweet Potato Soup Ⓖ Ⓢ

Serves 2 | Most sweet potato soups are flavored with nutmeg, cinnamon, and ginger, making them very reminiscent of butternut squash and pumpkin soups. That's tasty and all, but I wanted to warm things up a bit with a curry. The key here is to slowly roast the sweet potato in your oven. This allows the natural sugars to crystallize, which really helps bring out the rich sweet potato flavor. The nutty flavor and texture of the wild rice adds the perfect contrast to the sweet and creamy soup.

1 medium sweet potato
    or yam
½ sweet onion, chopped
3 garlic cloves, minced
1 c vegetable broth
½ to 1 tsp mild curry
    powder
¼ to ½ tsp garam masala
½ c non-dairy milk
¼ c cooked wild rice

CHEF'S NOTE:
*This recipe becomes
more flavorful
over time. If
possible, make a
day in advance and
gently reheat.*

1. Preheat oven to 425°F.
2. Bake sweet potato until fully cooked, about 45 minutes to 1 hour.
3. Allow potato to cool completely, then peel and discard the skin.
4. Transfer potato to a blender and set aside.
5. In a medium saucepan, combine onion, garlic, broth, ½ tsp of the curry, and ¼ tsp of the garam masala.
6. Bring to a boil, then reduce heat to low, cover, and simmer until onion is translucent, about 5 to 7 minutes.
7. Transfer onion mixture to the blender with the potato, add non-dairy milk and blend until smooth and creamy.
8. Return soup to saucepan and heat thoroughly.
9. Taste and adjust seasonings, adding ½ tsp of the curry or ¼ tsp more of the garam masala if desired.
10. If the soup becomes too thick, thin it out with a little non-dairy milk or water.
11. Ladle soup into bowls, adding warm rice into the center.
12. Sprinkle with ground cinnamon for garnish and serve.

NUTRITIONAL INFORMATION 🥄 Calories **186**; Calories from Fat **9**; Total Fat **1.0g**; Cholesterol **0mg**; Total Carbohydrate **39.7g**; Dietary Fiber **4.6g**; Sugars **4.0g**

Garden Chowder

Serves 2 | This *Gahden Chowdah* is wicked awesome. It embodies the creaminess of a true New England–style chowder but keeps it light and healthy with an abundance of vegetables.

1 tsp rubbed sage
(not powdered)
¼ tsp dried thyme
2 tbsp whole-wheat
pastry flour
2 tbsp nutritional yeast
1 c non-dairy milk
1 c vegetable broth
¼ tsp ground nutmeg
½ tsp granulated garlic
powder
½ tsp granulated onion
powder
½ c peeled and diced or
sliced carrot
1 c peeled and diced sweet
potato or yam
1 c frozen yellow corn
1 c chopped kale or spinach
1 tbsp ketchup
½ tsp pure maple syrup
salt, to taste
pepper, to taste

1. Grind sage and thyme with a mortar and pestle or with fingers so it's finer, like the consistency of coarse salt or finer.

2. Whisk flour, yeast, non-dairy milk, broth, sage, thyme, nutmeg, garlic powder, and onion powder together in a medium pot.

3. Add carrot, sweet potato or yam, and corn, then cover and bring to a boil.

4. Once it's boiling, add kale or spinach, cover again, and reduce heat to medium.

5. Continue to cook until kale or spinach is wilted and the other vegetables are fork-tender, about 5 to 7 minutes.

6. Remove from heat and stir in ketchup and maple syrup. Add salt and pepper.

7. If broth is too thick, thin out by adding ¼ to ½ cup of non-dairy milk.

> **CHEF'S NOTE:** *Gluten-free flours or blends may be substituted for the whole-wheat pastry flour in this recipe.*

NUTRITIONAL INFORMATION ✎ Calories **276**; Calories from Fat **25**; Total Fat **2.8g**; Cholesterol **0mg**; Total Carbohydrate **57.0g**; Dietary Fiber **8.5g**; Sugars **10.8g**; Protein **10.5g**

Red Lentil Dal

Serves 4 | *Pictured opposite* | Dals are essentially thick stews made with lentils and traditional Indian spices. On my website, Happyherbivore.com, this is one of my most popular recipes. It's been around the online block a few times, and for good reason. It's easy, delicious, and cheap. Make it once and it will never leave your regular rotation, I promise.

1 small onion, diced
2 garlic cloves, minced
1 tsp turmeric
1 tsp ground cumin
1 tsp paprika
1 tbsp ground ginger
½ c dried red lentils
2 c vegetable broth
1 chopped tomato with
  juices
3 oz tomato paste
  (about 5 tbsp)
1 tbsp ground coriander
2 tsp garam masala
salt, to taste
pepper, to taste
cayenne, to taste

1. Line a medium pot with ¼ cup of water and cook onions and garlic until translucent.

2. Add turmeric, cumin, paprika, and ginger and cook for another 2 minutes, adding water if necessary to prevent sticking or burning.

3. Add lentils, broth, tomato, tomato paste, and coriander, stirring to combine.

4. Bring to a boil, then reduce heat to low and simmer for 15 minutes or until lentils are cooked and orange-ish.

5. Add garam masala, stirring to combine, and let rest 5 minutes. Add salt, pepper, and cayenne.

CHEF'S NOTE: *If tomatoes are out of season, use ¼ cup of tomato sauce or two peeled canned tomatoes.*

NUTRITIONAL INFORMATION Calories **134**; Calories from Fat **7**; Total Fat **0.7g**; Cholesterol **0mg**; Total Carbohydrate **25.5g**; Dietary Fiber **9.3g**; Sugars **4.9g**; Protein **7.9g**

Yellow Dal

Makes 2 cups (2 servings) | This yellow dal is a quick and flavorful meal that pairs well with brown rice and cooked greens such as spinach.

1 c dried yellow split peas
1 tsp garam masala
½ tsp prepared yellow
   mustard
½ tsp turmeric
½ tsp ground cumin
¼ tsp ground ginger
⅛ to ¼ tsp cayenne powder
   or hot sauce
salt, to taste

1. Bring 2 cups of water to boil.
2. Add remaining ingredients except salt and reduce heat to low.
3. Cover and simmer for 30 minutes, or until most if not all of the water has been absorbed and the yellow split peas are soft but not mushy.
4. Add 1 to 4 tbsp more water so the mixture is a little wet.
5. Add salt.

NUTRITIONAL INFORMATION 🥄 Calories **345.5**; Calories from Fat **14**; Total Fat **1.5g**; Cholesterol **0mg**; Total Carbohydrate **61g**; Dietary Fiber **25.8g**; Sugars **0g**; Protein **24.5g**

Kik Alicha

Makes 2 cups (2 servings) | A mild Ethiopian dal made of yellow split peas. Serve with injera bread.

3 c vegetable broth or water
1 c dried yellow split peas
1 small onion, diced
3 garlic cloves, minced
½ tsp turmeric
¼ to ½ tsp Berberé (pg. 275),
   or to taste
¼ tsp ground ginger
¼ tsp mild curry powder
¼ tsp garam masala
salt, to taste
pepper, to taste

1. Bring 3 cups of broth or water to a boil and add split peas.

2. Bring to a boil again, cover, reduce heat to low, and simmer for 30 minutes, or until most of the liquid has been absorbed.

3. About 5 minutes before split peas are done, line a skillet with a thin layer of water and cook onion and garlic over high heat until onion is just translucent, about 3 minutes.

4. Add spices, stirring to combine and completely coat the onion.

5. Add onion mixture to split peas and simmer for another 5 minutes, stirring occasionally to prevent sticking or burning.

6. Taste; add another ⅛ to ¼ tsp of Berberé if desired.

7. Add salt and pepper.

8. Let rest for 5 minutes before serving.

NUTRITIONAL INFORMATION 🥄 Calories **360**; Calories from Fat **12**; Total Fat **1.3g**; Cholesterol **0mg**; Total Carbohydrate **64.9g**; Dietary Fiber **26.0g**; Sugars **9.4g**; Protein **25.0g**

Chana Palak Masala

Serves 4 | *Pictured opposite* | This spicy chickpea and spinach tomato stew is great for anyone trying Indian food for the first time. The flavors are familiar but still true to Indian cuisine. Serve with whole-wheat pitas, whole-wheat tortillas, or cooked brown rice for a complete meal.

1 small onion, diced
2 garlic cloves, minced
1 12-oz can peeled whole
  tomatoes with juices
1 15-oz can chickpeas,
  drained
1 12-oz bag baby spinach,
  fresh or frozen
1 c vegetable broth or water
½ tsp ground cumin
½ tsp ground coriander
½ tsp mild curry powder
½ tsp turmeric
¼ tsp ground ginger
red pepper flakes, as
  desired
½ to 1 tsp garam masala
1 tsp lemon juice (optional)

1. Line a large pot with a thin layer of water and cook onion and garlic over medium heat until translucent, about 3 minutes.

2. Add tomatoes with their juices, chickpeas, spinach, and broth, stirring to combine.

3. Cover and cook over medium heat until spinach cooks down, about 4 minutes.

4. Using a wooden spoon or firm spatula, break tomatoes apart.

5. Add remaining ingredients except garam masala, cover, and cook for 3 minutes more.

6. Add garam masala, stirring to combine, and cook for another 2 minutes.

7. Turn off heat and let sit for 5 minutes, allowing the flavors to merge.

NUTRITIONAL INFORMATION ✎ Calories **227**; Calories from Fat **31**; Total Fat **3.4g**; Cholesterol **0mg**; Total Carbohydrate **39.5g**; Dietary Fiber **11.5g**; Sugars **8.7g**; Protein **13.0g**

Rajma Masala

Serves 2 | *Pictured opposite* | This is a flavorful kidney bean curry, much like the Indian cousin to vegetarian chili.

1 medium onion, finely chopped
1 tsp ground coriander
1 tsp chili powder
1 tsp ground cumin
½ tsp turmeric
⅛ tsp ground ginger
1 8-oz can tomato sauce
1 c canned or cooked kidney beans
salt, to taste
1 tsp garam masala
fresh cilantro, chopped (for garnishing)
1 to 2 cups cooked basmati brown rice

1. Line a medium saucepan with a thin layer of water and cook onion over medium-high heat for 3 minutes.
2. Add coriander, chili powder, cumin, turmeric, and ginger, stirring to combine.
3. Continue to cook until almost all of the water has cooked off.
4. Add tomato sauce, kidney beans, and salt.
5. Lower heat to low-medium and cook until thoroughly warm.
6. Turn off heat, stir in garam masala, and let rest for 5 minutes, allowing flavors to merge.
7. Serve over rice and garnish with chopped fresh cilantro.

VARIATION

Spicy Rajma Masala ⬡ Ⓖ Ⓢ ✪ ✎ Add 1 4-oz can of diced green chilies and cayenne pepper or hot sauce to taste.

NUTRITIONAL INFORMATION

RAJMA MASALA ✎ Calories **312**; Calories from Fat **24**; Total Fat **2.7g**; Cholesterol **0mg**; Total Carbohydrate **64.0g**; Dietary Fiber **11.0g**; Sugars **8.6g**; Protein **13.2g**

SPICY RAJMA MASALA ✎ Calories **360**; Calories from Fat **30**; Total Fat **3.32g**; Cholesterol **0mg**; Total Carbohydrate **74.4g**; Dietary Fiber **13**; Sugars **8.6g**; Protein **14.8g**

Yemisir W'et Ⓕ Ⓖ Ⓢ

Makes 4 cups | A spicy Ethiopian red lentil stew. Serve with injera bread.

3 c vegetable broth or water
1 c dried red lentils
1 small onion, diced
3 garlic cloves, minced
2 tsp sweet paprika
1 tsp ground cumin
½ to 1 tsp Berberé (pg. 275),
   or to taste
¼ tsp ground ginger
4 to 6 tbsp tomato paste
1 15-oz can diced tomatoes,
   undrained
½ tsp garam masala
salt, to taste
pepper, to taste

1. Bring 3 cups of broth or water to a boil and add lentils.

2. Bring to a boil again, cover, reduce heat to low, and simmer for 30 minutes, or until most of the liquid has been absorbed and lentils are orange-ish.

3. About 5 minutes before lentils are done, line a skillet with a thin layer of water and cook onion and garlic over high heat until onion is just translucent, about 3 minutes.

4. Add paprika, cumin, ½ tsp of Berberé, and ginger, stirring to combine and completely coat the onions.

5. Add onion mixture, 4 tbsp of tomato paste, and tomatoes with juices to lentils and simmer another 10 minutes, stirring occasionally to prevent sticking or burning.

6. Add garam masala and stir to combine.

7. Taste, adding another ¼ to ½ tsp of Berberé and more tomato paste if desired.

8. Add salt and pepper.

9. Let rest for 5 minutes before serving.

NUTRITIONAL INFORMATION ✎ Calories **219**; Calories from Fat **8**; Total Fat **0.9g**; Cholesterol **0mg**; Total Carbohydrate **40.2g**; Dietary Fiber **17.8g**; Sugars **7.2g**; Protein **14.5g**

Chili sans Carne

Serves 8 | Thick and meaty, this chili is perfect on a cold winter day. Serve it with Cornbread (pg. 49) or Maple-Cornbread Biscuits (pg. 39) and use your leftovers to make Chili Enchiladas (pg. 106), Tex-Mex Chili Mac (pg. 156), or Cha-Cha Chili Nachos (pg. 246).

1 small onion, diced
1 28-oz can diced tomatoes
    with juices
2 tbsp chili powder,
    or to taste
1 tsp ground cumin
1 tsp dried oregano
1 tsp granulated garlic
    powder
1 15-oz can kidney beans,
    drained and rinsed
1 15-oz can pinto beans,
    drained and rinsed
1 c frozen yellow corn
1 tbsp ketchup
1 tbsp prepared yellow
    mustard
1 tsp pure maple syrup
1 tsp mild curry powder
1 tbsp Vegan Worcestershire
    Sauce (pg. 272)
1½ c TVP or TSP
2 c No-Beef Broth (pg. 279)
salt, to taste
pepper, to taste
cayenne powder, to taste
hot sauce, to taste

1. Line a medium pot with a thin layer of water.

2. Add onion and cook over medium heat until translucent and most of water has evaporated, about 3 minutes.

3. Add tomatoes with their juices, chili powder, cumin, oregano, and garlic and bring to a boil.

4. Once it's boiling, reduce heat to low, cover, and simmer for 30 to 45 minutes, until the liquid has reduced slightly.

5. Add beans, corn, ketchup, mustard, maple syrup, curry, and Vegan Worcestershire Sauce, stirring to combine.

6. Cover and turn off heat, but leave on the warm stove. Meanwhile, prepare broth.

7. Combine TVP with No-Beef Broth, then add to chili, stirring to combine.

8. Set aside uncovered for 10 minutes.

9. Give it a good stir, then add salt and pepper.

10. Add cayenne powder or hot sauce if desired, then serve.

NUTRITIONAL INFORMATION ← Calories **229**; Calories from Fat **14.9**; Fat **1.6g**; Cholesterol **0mg**; Total Carbohydrate **37.4g**; Dietary Fiber **11.7g**; Sugars **6.4g**; Protein **18.2g**

Cincinnati "Skyline" Chili

Serves 8 | *Pictured opposite* | Skyline chili was invented by Greek immigrant Nicholas Lambrinides in the heart of Cincinnati. Unlike Texas-style chili con carne, Skyline chili is made with chocolate, cinnamon, and traditional Greek spices and is served over hot dogs or spaghetti in five different ways.

1 yellow onion, diced
4 garlic cloves, minced
2 to 3 tbsp chili powder
1 tsp ground cumin
1 tsp ground cinnamon
½ tsp cayenne pepper
¼ tsp allspice
⅛ tsp ground cloves
2 tbsp unsweetened cocoa
2 c No-Beef Broth (pg. 279)
1 bay leaf
2 tsp Vegan Worcestershire
  Sauce (pg. 272)
1 15-oz can crushed
  tomatoes
1 c bulgur wheat
1 lb cooked whole-wheat
  spaghetti (2-way)
Cheddar Cheesy Sauce
  (pg. 264) (3-way)
1 white onion, diced (4-way)
1 15-oz can kidney beans,
  drained and rinsed
  (5-way)

1. Line a medium pot with a thin layer of water and cook yellow onion and garlic until onion is translucent, about 3 minutes.

2. Whisk spices and cocoa together with broth until evenly incorporated and add to saucepan.

3. Add bay leaf, Vegan Worcestershire Sauce, tomatoes, and bulgur wheat, stirring to combine.

4. Bring to a near boil over high heat, then cover and reduce heat to low.

5. Simmer for 20 to 30 minutes, until bulgur is cooked.

6. Add additional water or broth if necessary to thin out chili.

7. Serve as follows: 1-way (just the chili), chili over spaghetti or a vegan hot dog (2-way), 2-way topped with Cheesy Sauce (3-way), 3-way topped with diced raw white onion (4-way), or 4-way topped with kidney beans (5-way).

CHEF'S NOTE: *You can substitute TVP Beef Crumbles (pg. 140) for the bulgur wheat (omitting broth) or reconstitute 1 cup of TVP with the broth instead. You can also use shredded vegan cheddar cheese instead of the cheese sauce if you prefer.*

NUTRITIONAL INFORMATION (CALCULATED 1-WAY) Calories **122**; Calories from Fat **8**; Total Fat **0.9g**; Cholesterol **0mg**; Total Carbohydrate **26.8g**; Dietary Fiber **5.3g**; Sugars **4.3g**; Protein **4.6g**

Burgers, Wraps, Tacos, & More

Black Bean Burgers

Makes 3 burgers | *Pictured opposite* | I love a good and quick meal, and this burger fits the bill perfectly. Serve with Rustic Yam Fries (pg. 179).

1 15-oz can black beans, drained and rinsed
¼ c fresh cilantro, minced
1 tsp ground cumin
½ tsp dried oregano
cayenne, to taste
salt, to taste
pepper, to taste
Breadcrumbs (pg. 284)
3 whole-wheat hamburger buns

1. Preheat oven to 350°F. Grease cookie sheet or line with parchment paper and set aside.

2. Pulse beans in food processor until mashed well or mash manually using a potato masher or fork.

3. Transfer to a mixing bowl and stir in cilantro and spices plus salt and pepper.

4. Add Breadcrumbs as necessary until the mixture can be handled and isn't terribly sticky, about ¼ cup.

5. If after ¼ cup it's still too sticky and difficult to work with, place in fridge 5 to 10 minutes.

6. Shape mixture into 3 patties.

7. Lightly spray each patty with cooking spray and bake 7 minutes.

8. Flip, re-spray, and bake for 7 to 10 minutes more until crisp on the outside and thoroughly warm.

9. Serve immediately on buns. Because there is no oil, these patties dry out as they sit so eat them right away.

NUTRITIONAL INFORMATION Calories **147**; Calories from Fat **14**; Total Fat **1.6g**; Cholesterol **0mg**; Total Carbohydrate **24.1g**; Dietary Fiber **7.5g**; Sugars **0.6g**; Protein **9.0g**

Mushroom Burgers

Makes 7 burgers | *Pictured opposite* | These burgers rock. They're perfect for backyard barbecues with friends, pool parties, or anytime you just want to sink your teeth into a meaty and juicy burger. The secret ingredient is the mushrooms, which naturally add a beefy flavor and hold in moisture. Top with all your favorite fixings and serve with Baked Onion Rings (pg. 176) or Rustic Yam Fries (pg. 179).

1 slice whole-wheat bread
8 oz cremini mushrooms
1 15-oz can pinto or kidney
    beans, drained
1 tsp paprika
1 tsp granulated onion
    powder
1 tsp granulated garlic
    powder
⅓ c vital wheat gluten
2 tbsp soy sauce
2 tbsp steak sauce
2 tbsp BBQ sauce
pepper, to taste

1. Preheat oven to 450°F. Grease or line a baking sheet with parchment paper.

2. Place bread slice in a food processor and allow the motor to run until breadcrumbs form. Transfer to a mixing bowl.

3. Place whole mushrooms in the food processor and pulse until coarsely shredded to the size of sliced olives. Transfer to a mixing bowl.

4. Repeat with pinto or kidney beans.

5. Combine all ingredients.

6. Using your hands, form 7 patties.

7. Place patties on cookie sheet, spray with cooking spray, and bake for 10 minutes.

8. Flip, re-spray, and bake for another 8 minutes.

9. Flip, re-spray for a third time, and bake 5 minutes more.

> **CHEF'S NOTE:** *You can also pan-fry or grill these burgers. Cook in a nonstick skillet, flipping every minute or so, until brown on each side. To grill, cook on foil until firm, then cook directly on grill until thoroughly heated. Once firm, remove foil and cook on rack to get a nice charcoal grill flavoring.*

NUTRITIONAL INFORMATION ⬧ Calories **113**; Calories from Fat **6**; Total Fat **0.7g**; Cholesterol **0mg**; Total Carbohydrate **17.5g**; Dietary Fiber **3.5g**; Sugars **3.7g**; Protein **8.4g**

Soul Burgers

Makes 4 burgers | These burgers are inspired by the key ingredients in soul food. They're hearty and a little spicy. Serve with Rustic Yam Fries (pg. 179) or Low-Country Cucumber Salad (pg. 186).

1 15-oz can black-eyed peas, drained and rinsed
½ small onion
1 jalapeño, seeded
1 red bell pepper, seeded and diced
1 tbsp ketchup
2 tsp prepared yellow mustard
½ tsp granulated garlic powder
½ tsp chili powder
½ tsp ground cumin
½ tsp dried thyme
¼ tsp salt
¼ tsp pepper
¼ tsp paprika
cayenne, to taste
Breadcrumbs (pg. 284), as necessary
4 whole-wheat buns

1. Preheat oven to 350°F. Grease cookie sheet or line with parchment paper and set aside.

2. Pulse black-eyed peas, onion, and jalapeño in food processor until coarsely ground.

3. Transfer to a mixing bowl and stir in bell pepper, ketchup, spices, thyme, salt, and pepper.

4. Add Breadcrumbs as necessary until the mixture can be handled and isn't terribly sticky, about ¼ to ½ cup.

5. If after ½ cup it's still too sticky and difficult to work with, place in fridge for 5 to 10 minutes.

6. Shape into 4 patties.

7. Lightly spray each patty with cooking spray and bake for 7 minutes.

8. Flip, re-spray, and bake for 7 minutes more.

9. Flip and re-spray a third time, baking for 7 to 10 minutes or until crisp on the outside and thoroughly warm.

10. Serve immediately on buns. Because there is no oil, these patties dry out as they sit so eat them right away.

NUTRITIONAL INFORMATION 🥄 Calories **113**; Calories from Fat **13**; Total Fat **1.4g**; Cholesterol **0mg**; Total Carbohydrate **20.5g**; Dietary Fiber **4.9g**; Sugars **3.8g**; Protein **6.6g**

BBQ Chop Wrap

Serves 1 | Cool, crisp, and so refreshing! For a more complex wrap, add Ranch Dip (pg. 232). Leftover Crispy Tortilla Sticks (pg. 239) can be substituted for the corn chips.

2 c chopped romaine
    lettuce
1 small tomato, diced
¼ c canned or cooked
    black beans
¼ c frozen yellow corn,
    thawed
2 tbsp BBQ sauce
1 whole-wheat wrap
    or corn tortilla
¼ c crumbled baked
    corn chips

1. Toss the lettuce, tomatoes, beans, corn, and BBQ sauce together in a mixing bowl, ensuring everything is mostly coated with BBQ sauce.
2. Scoop into wrap.
3. Add corn chips over top and roll up.

NUTRITIONAL INFORMATION 🥄 Calories **167**; Calories from Fat **12**; Total Fat **1.4g**; Cholesterol **0mg**; Total Carbohydrate **34.5g**; Dietary Fiber **6.6g**; Sugars **13.9g**; Protein **6.5g**

Salsa Chickpea Lettuce Wraps

Makes 10 wraps | *Pictured opposite* | I munch on these wraps all summer long when it's too hot to cook and I want nothing but cool, refreshing foods. I also love to try out different fruit-based salsas with this recipe to keep it new and exciting each time I make it.

1 15-oz can chickpeas,
   drained and rinsed
1 12-oz jar salsa
10 lettuce leaves
2 bell peppers, seeded and
   finely chopped (optional)

1. Combine chickpeas and salsa in a medium saucepan.
2. Cook over medium-high heat, stirring occasionally, until all of the liquid has been absorbed and the chickpeas have taken on the salsa's color, about 8 minutes.
3. For best results, refrigerate overnight.
4. Spoon chickpeas into lettuce leaves and top with chopped bell pepper pieces.
5. Serve chilled, warm, or at room temperature.

NUTRITIONAL INFORMATION 🥄 Calories **51**; Calories from Fat **4**; Total Fat **0.4g**; Cholesterol **0mg**; Total Carbohydrate **9.8g**; Dietary Fiber **0.6g**; Sugars **3.2g**; Protein **2.6g**

Smoky Black Bean Wraps

Serves 2 | *Pictured opposite* | This is my husband's all-time favorite wrap. It's smoky and a little spicy, perfect for lunch or a quick dinner.

3 tbsp Mayo (pg. 271)
1 tsp liquid smoke
½ tsp chipotle powder
⅛ tsp paprika
salt, to taste
pepper, to taste
2 large whole-wheat wraps
   or corn tortillas
1 15-oz can black beans,
   drained and rinsed
2 c arugula or chopped
   lettuoo
1 large tomato, seeded
   and diced

1. Combine Mayo, liquid smoke, chipotle powder, and paprika.

2. Add salt and pepper.

3. Spread Mayo mixture on wraps in a thin but generous layer and top with beans, arugula or lettuce, and tomatoes.

4. Roll up and enjoy.

NUTRITIONAL INFORMATION 🥄 Calories **217**; Calories from Fat **18**; Total Fat **2.0g**; Cholesterol **0mg**; Total Carbohydrate **36.8g**; Dietary Fiber **11.3g**; Sugars **4.3g**; Protein **14.3g**

Wizard Roll-Ups

Serves 2 | Nothing short of a jazzed-up bean burrito, wizard roll-ups are my go-to meal on nights I'm not in the mood to cook. This my basic template—I won't even call it a recipe—works with every kind of bean and salsa combination you can come up with. Stir in any leftover veggies and grains you have on hand and let the wizard work his magic on your leftovers.

1 15-oz can pinto beans, drained and rinsed
2 tbsp salsa, or to taste
leftover vegetables or grains
2 whole-wheat wraps or corn tortillas

1. Combine pinto beans with 2 tbsp of salsa in food processor. Pulse or allow the motor to run until the beans are chunky or pureed, your choice.

2. Add more salsa if necessary or desired, but be careful not to make it too watery. If using pinto beans and traditional tomato-based salsa, the mixture should be a bit pink.

3. Mix in leftover grains or veggies, or puree them with the beans.

4. Slather into warmed wraps, roll up, and enjoy!

NUTRITIONAL INFORMATION 🥄 Calories **184**; Calories from Fat **15**; Total Fat **1.7g**; Cholesterol **0mg**; Total Carbohydrate **30.4g**; Dietary Fiber **10.1g**; Sugars **2.1g**; Protein **10.1g**

Blue Corn Chickpea Tacos

Makes 8 tacos | *Pictured on pg. 99 (with TVP Tacos)* | Everyone loves these tacos. I've managed to get my parents, my best friend, and just about everyone I know hooked on them. They're also one of the most popular recipes on my website, Happyherbivore.com. I like to eat these chickpeas in blue corn taco shells with arugula, fresh tomatoes, and a tiny dollop of Sour Cream (pg. 271) on top.

1 tbsp soy sauce
1 to 2 tsp lemon or lime juice
1 tbsp chili powder
1½ tsp ground cumin
1 tsp fine salt
1 tsp pepper
½ tsp paprika
¼ tsp granulated garlic powder
¼ tsp granulated onion powder
⅛ tsp cayenne powder
¼ tsp dried marjoram or oregano
1 15-oz can chickpeas, drained and rinsed
blue corn taco shells
arugula or lettuce
1 salad tomato, diced

1. Preheat oven to 400°F.
2. Grease cookie sheet or line with parchment paper and set aside.
3. Whisk soy sauce, juice, and spices together, then combine with chickpeas in a bowl, stirring to combine.
4. Transfer to cookie sheet in a single layer.
5. Spray with cooking spray and bake for 20 to 40 minutes, until chickpeas are as crisp as desired.
6. Spoon chickpeas into taco shells and top with greens and tomatoes.

NUTRITIONAL INFORMATION 🥄 Calories **59**; Calories from Fat **6**; Total Fat **0.7g**; Cholesterol **0mg**; Total Carbohydrate **10.6g**; Dietary Fiber **0.6g**; Sugars **2.7g**; Protein **3.1g**

TVP Tacos

Makes 4 tacos | *Pictured opposite* | Crunchy taco shells, juicy and tasty beef—or chicken-style TVP, lettuce, and tomatoes . . . Who doesn't look forward to taco night? I like to eat my tacos with hot sauce, and my husband likes to smear a thin layer of Mayo (pg. 271) inside the shells before stuffing. You can also substitute Mexican Chorizo (pg. 147) for the meat and load the taco with chopped cabbage instead of lettuce.

BEEF STYLE:
¾ c No-Beef Broth (pg. 279)
2 tbsp steak sauce
2 tbsp low-sodium soy sauce
2 tbsp onion flakes
4 tsp chili powder
2 tsp granulated garlic powder
1 tsp ground cumin
hot sauce or cayenne powder, as desired
1 c textured vegetable protein (TVP)
4 taco shells

CHICKEN STYLE:
1 c No-Chicken Broth (pg. 281)
2 tsp Vegetarian Chicken Broth
   Powder (pg. 281)
1 tsp granulated onion powder
2 tsp granulated garlic powder
2 tsp chili powder
1 tsp ground cumin
lime juice, as desired
1 c textured vegetable protein (TVP)
4 taco shells

1. Bring broth to a boil.
2. Turn off heat and add remaining ingredients up to, but not including, TVP, stirring to incorporate.
3. Add TVP, cover, and let TVP soak up all the liquid, about 5 minutes. Stir if necessary.
4. Once TVP is reconstituted, serve ¼ cup of reconstituted TVP in each taco shell. Add desired fillings, such as lettuce and tomato.

NUTRITIONAL INFORMATION

BEEF TVP TACOS 🥢 Calories **115**; Calories from Fat **5**; Total Fat **0.6g**; Cholesterol **0mg**; Total Carbohydrate **14.2g**; Dietary Fiber **5.4g**; Sugars **6.3g**; Protein **13.5g**

CHICKEN TVP TACOS 🥢 Calories **103**; Calories from Fat **3**; Total Fat **0.4g**; Cholesterol **0mg**; Total Carbohydrate **11.9g**; Dietary Fiber **4.7g**; Sugars **3.9g**; Protein **12.7g**

2-Layer Tacos

Makes 8 tacos | This taco is the best of both worlds. You get the bean burrito *and* the savory taco, as well as the warm soft shell *and* the crunch.

1 recipe TVP Tacos (pg. 98)
  or Chickpea Tacos
  (pg. 97)
8 whole-wheat tortillas,
  warmed
1 15-oz can vegetarian
  refried beans

1. Prepare 8 TVP or Chickpea Tacos.
2. Gently warm the tortillas.
3. Spoon a thin layer of refried beans in the center, leaving a 1-inch edge.
4. Wrap the tortillas around the crunchy taco shells, making the beans the glue between the two shells.

NUTRITIONAL INFORMATION 🥢 Calories **107**; Calories from Fat **2**; Total Fat **0.2g**; Cholesterol **0mg**; Total Carbohydrate **16.2g**; Dietary Fiber **5.3g**; Sugars **2.0g**; Protein **10.2g**

Baked Chimichangas

Makes 4 | *Pictured on pg. 84* | Chimichangas are deep-fried burritos commonly made with beans, rice, cheese, and ground meat and topped with sour cream, guacamole, and salsa. This recipe is along that same line but doesn't have to be. Make your own variation by substituting leftover Charleston Red Rice (pg. 192) for the brown rice, try out different beans or use refried beans, add diced green chilies or jalapeños for a kick, add chopped lettuce or cabbage, include diced tomatoes or vegetables, substitute the chickpeas from the Chickpea Tacos instead of the TVP meat, or pour Enchilada Sauce (pg. 260), Mexican Queso Sauce (variation, pg. 263), or Quick Queso Sauce (pg. 263) over the top before serving. Any combination is a good one; don't be afraid to get creative!

1 c cooked brown rice
1 15-oz can pinto beans,
  drained and rinsed
1 recipe TVP Tacos
  (pg. 98), minus the shells
  or Mexican Chorizo
  (pg. 147)
salsa
8 whole-wheat wraps or
  large tortillas
Low-Fat Guacamole
  (pg. 231)
Sour Cream (pg. 271)

1. Preheat oven to 450°F. Grease cookie sheet or line with parchment paper and set aside.

2. Spoon rice, beans, TVP Tacos meat or Mexican Chorizo, and a little salsa into the center of each wrap. Fold wraps chimichanga-style (close both ends and shape like a rectangle).

3. Transfer to cookie sheet and spray with cooking spray.

4. Bake for 15 to 25 minutes, until wraps are crisp and golden but not burnt.

5. Re-spray halfway through baking if necessary.

6. Once plated, top with Low-Fat Guacamole, Sour Cream, and salsa.

NUTRITIONAL INFORMATION 🥄 Calories **261**; Calories from Fat **15**; Total Fat **1.7g**; Cholesterol **0mg**; Total Carbohydrate **41.2g**; Dietary Fiber **11.2g**; Sugars **6.2g**; Protein **19.5g**

Steak and Pepper Fajitas

Makes 6 fajitas | *Pictured opposite* | Using different colors of bell peppers makes this dish absolutely stunning. You can also substitute 1 to 2 additional bell peppers in place of the mushrooms if you prefer.

2 recipes Portobello Steaks
   (pg. 148)
3 bell peppers, seeded
1 onion
1 tbsp cornstarch
1 tbsp chili powder
1 tsp fine salt
1 tsp paprika
1 tsp raw sugar (optional)
¼ tsp granulated onion
   powder
¼ tsp granulated garlic
   powder
¼ tsp ground cumin
 hot sauce, to taste
6 whole-wheat wraps or
   large tortillas
shredded lettuce or
   cabbage (optional)

1. Cut the prepared portobellos into ⅓-inch-wide strips and set aside.

2. Cut bell peppers into ½-inch strips and set aside.

3. Cut the onion into ¼-inch strips and set aside.

4. In a bowl, whisk remaining ingredients, except tortilla and lettuce or cabbage, with ⅓ cup of water and set aside.

5. Line a medium skillet with a thin layer of water.

6. Add prepared strips of onion and peppers and cook over medium heat, adding water as necessary, until the peppers are cooked but still crisp and no additional water remains, about 3 to 5 minutes.

7. Re-whisk spice mixture and pour over peppers and onion.

8. Allow the mixture to slightly thicken for 1 to 2 minutes, then stir to combine so peppers and onion are evenly coated.

9. Spoon peppers and onion into wraps, add portobello slices and lettuce or cabbage, if using, and serve.

NUTRITIONAL INFORMATION ✎ Calories **71**; Calories from Fat **6**; Total Fat **0.7g**; Cholesterol **0mg**; Total Carbohydrate **13.4g**; Dietary Fiber **3.6g**; Sugars **5.5g**; Protein **3.2g**

Smoky Black Bean Enchiladas

Makes 8 enchiladas | *Pictured opposite* | For the last year it's been my husband's personal mission to slip liquid smoke into everything we eat. One night he added a little liquid smoke into our basic enchilada recipe, and wow! The liquid smoke took these enchiladas from good to freakin' outstanding. Thanks, baby!

1 lb extra-firm tofu, drained and crumbled
1 15-oz can black beans, drained and rinsed
1 to 2 tbsp chili powder
2 tsp liquid smoke
1 tsp granulated garlic powder
hot sauce, to taste
8 whole-wheat wraps or corn tortillas
Enchilada Sauce (pg. 260)
1 4-oz can black olives, sliced
Quick Queso Sauce (pg. 263)

1. Preheat oven to 350°F.
2. Crumble tofu in a large bowl.
3. Add beans, chili powder, liquid smoke, garlic, and hot sauce as desired.
4. Mix until evenly incorporated.
5. Spoon filling into wraps, fold over, and place in an oven-safe dish crease side down.
6. Pour enchilada sauce over the wraps, reserving about 1 cup of liquid for serving if desired.
7. Sprinkle olives over top and bake for 15 to 30 minutes, less time for a soft shell and longer for a more crisp shell.
8. Meanwhile, prepare Quick Queso Sauce and then spoon it over top before serving.

NUTRITIONAL INFORMATION ✎ Calories **89**; Calories from Fat **22**; Total Fat **2.5g**; Cholesterol **0mg**; Total Carbohydrate **9.8g**; Dietary Fiber **3.2g**; Sugars **0.6g**; Protein **7.3g**

Chili Enchiladas

Makes 8 | Leftover Chili sans Carne (pg. 81) provides a meaty and flavorful enchilada filling.

2 c Chili sans Carne (pg. 81)
8 whole-wheat or corn tortillas
1 recipe Enchilada Sauce (pg. 260)
1 4-oz can sliced black olives, drained (optional)
1 recipe Cheddar Cheesy Sauce (pg. 269) or Quick Queso Sauce (pg. 263)

1. Preheat oven to 350°F.

2. Spoon ¼ cup of Chili sans Carne filling into tortillas, fold over, and place in an oven-safe dish crease side down.

3. Pour Enchilada Sauce over the tortillas, reserving about 1 cup of liquid for serving if desired.

4. Sprinkle olives over top, if using, and bake for 15 to 30 minutes, less for a soft shell and more for a crispier shell.

5. Spoon Cheddar Cheesy Sauce or Quick Queso Sauce over top before serving.

NUTRITIONAL INFORMATION 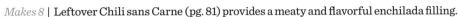 Calories **197.9**; Calories from Fat **30.8**; Total Fat **3.4g**; Cholesterol **0mg**; Total Carbohydrate **33.8g**; Dietary Fiber **6.1g**; Sugars **4.1g**; Protein **10g**

PB&F

Serves 1 | A PB&F, which stands for "peanut butter and fruit," is a delicious alternative to the traditional PB&J because it is lower in fat, calories, and sugar.

2 slices whole-wheat bread
3 to 4 tbsp Nutty Spread
   (pg. 253)
fresh banana or apple slices
1 tbsp agave nectar
   (optional)

1. Toast bread, if desired.
2. Generously smear Nutty Spread along one slice of bread.
3. Add banana or apple slices on top and drizzle agave over top if using.
4. Place remaining bread slice on top and gently press down to close the sandwich.

VARIATIONS

Fluffy Nutty Substitute Ricemellow for the fresh fruit and omit the agave.

Ants on Toast Toast bread, add 2 tbsp of raisins or other dried fruit, and drizzle with pure maple syrup instead of agave.

Creamy Nutty Toast bread, smear vegan cream cheese on the other slice of toast, and omit fruit and agave.

NUTRITIONAL INFORMATION (USING 1 BANANA) Calories **240**; Calories from Fat **59**; Total Fat **6.5g**; Cholesterol **0mg**; Total Carbohydrate **42.9g**; Dietary Fiber **6.8g**; Sugars **6.8g**; Protein **7g**

Meatball Subs

Makes 8 sandwiches | *Pictured opposite with Meatless Balls* | Leftover meatballs belong in a sandwich! Meatball subs are also terrific party foods that go over well with kids, omnivores, and picky vegan foodies alike.

Creole Roasted Red-Pepper
    Sauce (pg. 257) or your
    favorite marinara
Veggie Croquettes (pg. 153)
    or Meatless Balls (pg. 165)
whole-wheat hot dog buns

1 Gently warm Creole Roasted Red-Pepper Sauce over medium heat.

2 Add Veggie Croquettes or Meatless Balls and allow to warm thoroughly over low heat, but do not bring to a boil.

3 Spoon into toasted buns and serve.

> **CHEF'S NOTE:** *If you're serving these at a party, heat the meatballs and marinara together in a slow-cooker on low. This way guests can help themselves to a hot sub throughout the game.*

NUTRITIONAL INFORMATION 🐟 Calories **224**; Calories from Fat **24.3**; Fat **2.7g**; Cholesterol **0mg**; Total Carbohydrate **34.5g**; Dietary Fiber **4.9g**; Sugars **7.1g**; Protein **13.8g**

Tempeh Joes

Makes 6 Sandwiches | Pictured opposite | Don't be surprised if Tempeh Joe becomes your new boyfriend. You can substitute another 1 cup cooked brown rice for the tempeh if you want a truly fat-free and soy-free joe, but you'll have to call him Rice Joe or Nice Joe instead. A diced green bell pepper and onion cooked in water or broth also make a nice addition to the mixture, extending the servings to 8 to 10 sandwiches.

1 8-oz package tempeh
1 tbsp soy sauce
1 c cooked brown rice
¼ c ketchup
2 tsp chili powder
1 tsp paprika
2 tsp prepared yellow
   mustard
hot sauce, to taste (optional)
salt, to taste (optional)
pepper, to taste (optional)
6 lettuce wraps or whole-
   wheat buns

1. Bring a pot of water, enough to completely submerge the tempeh, approximately 2 to 4 cups, to a boil.
2. Add tempeh and soy sauce and bring to a boil again.
3. Boil for 10 minutes, then drain and rinse with cold water until the tempeh is warm.
4. Shred tempeh using the shredding attachment for your food processor or a cheese grater. You want the tempeh to be granulated and slightly larger but similar in shape to the rice.
5. Combine tempeh with remaining ingredients except salt and pepper in a large bowl, stirring to combine.
6. Salt and pepper if desired.
7. Spoon into lettuce wraps or onto a whole-wheat bun.

NUTRITIONAL INFORMATION 🥄 Calories **131.3**; Calories from Fat **31.7**; Fat **3.5g**; Cholesterol **0mg**; Protein **7.6g**; Carbohydrate **18.1g**; Dietary Fiber **5.6g**; Sugar **0g**

"Tuna" Salad

Makes 4 sandwiches | *Pictured opposite* | It's amazing how chickpeas and a little kelp recreate the taste of tuna. This salad is great on whole-wheat bread, smashed in a lettuce wrap, or served over a warm whole-wheat English muffin and topped with a slice of tomato.

1 15-oz can chickpeas,
   drained and rinsed
2 celery stalks, washed
1 to 2 tbsp pickle relish
½ tsp onion flakes
2 tsp nutritional yeast
1 tbsp soy sauce
3 tbsp Mayo (pg. 271)
½ tsp kelp powder
⅛ tsp lemon juice (optional)
pepper, to taste

1. In a large mixing bowl, mash chickpeas with a fork until coarse and no whole beans are left. Alternatively, pulse beans in a food processor a few times, careful not to puree, and transfer to a mixing bowl.

2. Shred celery with a cheese grater or mince in food processor by letting the motor run.

3. Transfer to the mixing bowl and add remaining ingredients, stirring to combine. Add more Mayo or kelp as necessary or desired.

VARIATION

Mediterranean Tuna Salad Stir in diced zucchini, tomatoes, red bell peppers, green bell peppers, red onions, and sliced black olives.

NUTRITIONAL INFORMATION Calories **125**; Calories from Fat 8; Total Fat **0.9g**; Cholesterol **0mg**; Total Carbohydrate **22.6g**; Dietary Fiber **4.4g**; Sugars **3.0g**; Protein **7.1g**

Quick
One-Pot
Dinners

Buddha's Delight

Serves 4 | If there were one dish I had to use to "convert" anyone to a vegan diet, this would be it. It's healthy, tasty, easy to make, beautiful, and an overall crowd-pleaser.

1 small onion, thinly sliced
2 garlic cloves, minced
½ c thinly sliced carrots
1 c shredded cabbage
½ c cauliflower florets
1 red bell pepper, seeded
　　and sliced
1 green bell pepper, seeded
　　and sliced
2 tbsp soy sauce
2 tbsp raw sugar
2 c cooked brown rice

1. Cook onion in ¼ cup of water over high heat.

2. Once onion is translucent, add remaining vegetables.

3. Reduce heat to medium and continue to cook, adding a little water as necessary until vegetables are cooked but still crisp, about 10 to 15 minutes.

4. Meanwhile, mix soy sauce and sugar together and pour over vegetables, stirring to coat.

5. Cook for another 5 minutes, then remove from heat and serve over a bed of cooked brown rice.

CHEF'S NOTE: *Feel free to add in broccoli florets, snow peas, sugar snap peas, mushrooms, bean sprouts, tofu chunks, edamame, or any other vegetables you have on hand or enjoy in stir-fries.*

NUTRITIONAL INFORMATION ← Calories **179**; Calories from Fat **10**; Total Fat **1.1g**; Cholesterol **0mg**; Total Carbohydrate **38.5g**; Dietary Fiber **4.5g**; Sugars **11.2g**; Protein **4.2g**

Cheater Pad Thai

Serves 2 | *Pictured on pg. 114* | I call this "cheater" because it's ridiculously easy and quick to make and also because this recipe uses 1 tbsp of peanut butter, so it's not fat-free. For an even lower-fat pad Thai, prepare the Nutty Spread (pg. 253) without cinnamon and use 1 to 2 tbsp in place of the peanut butter.

¼ lb thick rice noodles
2 tbsp soy sauce
1 tbsp smooth peanut butter
1 tbsp sweet red chili Asian sauce
¼ tsp granulated garlic powder
¼ tsp ground ginger
¼ tsp hot sauce, or to taste
3 oz bean sprouts

CHEF'S NOTE:
Letting this sauce rest for a few minutes is a great way to intensify the flavor.

1. Prepare rice noodles according to package directions.
2. In a small bowl, whisk 2 tbsp of warm water, soy sauce, peanut butter, chili sauce, garlic powder, ginger, and hot sauce together until combined. It may appear too runny at first, but it's not.
3. Taste, adding more hot sauce if desired.
4. Using tongs, toss prepared noodles with your newly created pad Thai sauce until all noodles are evenly coated.
5. Plate and top with bean sprouts.
6. Garnish with chopped raw peanuts and a lime wedge if desired.

VARIATIONS

Lower-Calorie Pad Thai For a lower-carbohydrate and lower-calorie pad Thai, substitute 2 cups of thinly sliced blanched cabbage for half of the rice noodles.

Vegetable Pad Thai Double the sauce; Cook 1 15-oz package of frozen stir-fry veggies according to package instructions and toss with sauce and noodles.

NUTRITIONAL INFORMATION Calories **283**; Calories from Fat **38**; Total Fat **4.3g**; Cholesterol **0mg**; Total Carbohydrate **55.0g**; Dietary Fiber **2.7g**; Sugars **4.1g**; Protein **7.9g**

Chickpeas and Dumplings

Serves 2 | *Pictured opposite* | A healthy and legume-filled version of chicken and dumplings.

1 c whole-wheat pastry
   flour
1 tsp fine salt
1 tbsp cornstarch
1 c No-Chicken Broth
   (pg. 281)
1 onion, diced
2 garlic cloves, minced
1 c brown mushrooms,
   thinly sliced (optional)
1 tbsp Poultry Seasoning
   Mix (pg. 273)
½ tsp dried thyme
½ tsp mild curry powder
⅛ tsp ground nutmeg
⅛ to 1 c non-dairy milk
2 tbsp nutritional yeast
1 c canned or cooked
   chickpeas
salt, to taste
pepper, to taste

CHEF'S NOTE:
*I've had mixed
results making
dumplings with
gluten-free flours.*

1. In a medium bowl, whisk flour with 1 tsp of salt until well combined.

2. Add 6 tbsp of cold water, stirring to make a ball.

3. Using your hands, knead a few times.

4. Flatten the dough out and, using a sharp knife, cut approximately 20 gnocchi-sized pillows and set aside.

5. Mix cornstarch into 2 tbsp of water and set aside.

6. Line a medium pot with a thin layer of No-Chicken Broth and cook the onion and garlic until translucent, about 3 minutes.

7. Add mushrooms and spices, continuing to cook until the mushrooms are soft and releasing juices, about 5 minutes, adding remaining broth as needed.

8. Then add ½ cup of non-dairy milk and immediately whisk in nutritional yeast.

9. Allow the mixture to come to a near boil, then add dumplings and bring to a boil again.

10. Once boiling, reduce heat to medium and keep cooking, stirring if necessary, until the dumplings start to float and are less doughy, about 4 minutes.

11. Add chickpeas and cornstarch mixture and continue to cook until chickpeas are thoroughly warm and liquid has thickened.

12. Thin out mixture with remaining non-dairy milk if desired or necessary.

13. Add salt and pepper to taste and serve.

NUTRITIONAL INFORMATION ⬳ Calories **469.5**; Calories from Fat **29.5**; Total Fat **3.3g**; Cholesterol **0mg**; Total Carbohydrate **91.5g**; Dietary Fiber **17g**; Sugars **2.3g**; Protein **20.1g**

Creole Black-Eyed Peas

Serves 2 | *Pictured opposite* | New Year's gets a Cajun-inspired makeover. Serve with Spicy Greens (pg. 184), Cornbread (pg. 49), and sliced Spicy Sausage (pg. 150).

Creole Roasted Red-Pepper
    Sauce (pg. 257)
1 c cooked black-eyed peas
1 c cooked brown rice
    or pearl barley

1. Prepare Creole Roasted Red-Pepper Sauce.

2. Stir black-eyed peas into the sauce and heat until thoroughly warm, about 3 to 5 minutes.

3. Line the bottom of two wide bowls with the sauce.

4. Pack the cooked rice or barley into a ½-cup measuring cup and then flip out into the center of the plate or bowl for a stunning presentation. Alternately, serve the sauce over the cooked rice or barley.

CHEF'S NOTE: *For a more authentic sauce, add 1 celery stalk, diced, and 1 large carrot, peeled and diced, with the onions to complete the holy trinity. You may also substitute 1¼ cups of diced canned tomatoes for the red bell peppers.*

NUTRITIONAL INFORMATION ➾ Calories **242**; Calories from Fat **19**; Total Fat **2.1g**; Cholesterol **0mg**; Total Carbohydrate **49.2g**; Dietary Fiber **7.6g**; Sugars **7.2g**; Protein **9.6g**

5-Spice Harmony Bowl

Serves 2 | *Pictured opposite* | Macro Bowls, short for macrobiotic bowls, are popping up on menus everywhere, particularly on the West Coast. They're usually composed of warm whole grains, leafy green vegetables, and another vegetable or beans. This combination follows the principles of macrobiotics, a diet that focuses on eating foods that create balance in the body. Inner harmony has never tasted so good.

1 c vegetable broth
1 tsp Chinese 5-spice powder
½ tsp granulated garlic powder
½ tsp ground ginger
1 medium sweet potato, peeled and diced
1 tbsp cornstarch mixed into 2 tbsp water
1 10-oz package frozen turnip greens, or other greens
salt, if desired
1 c cooked wild rice

1. Whisk broth, 5-spice powder, garlic powder, and ginger together.
2. Transfer to a skillet and add sweet potato.
3. Bring to a boil over high heat and continue to cook until potatoes are fork-tender, about 3 to 8 minutes.
4. Add cornstarch mixture and allow the sauce to thicken for about 1 minute.
5. Turn off heat, cover, and set aside.
6. Cook greens according to directions, squeezing out any excess water. Sprinkle with salt if desired.
7. Plate greens, then add ½ cup of cooked rice on top of each plate.
8. Give the sweet potato mixture a good stir, then scoop half onto each plate and serve.

NUTRITIONAL INFORMATION 🐘 Calories **196**; Calories from Fat **9**; Total Fat **1.0g**; Cholesterol **0mg**; Total Carbohydrate **41.4g**; Dietary Fiber **6.7g**; Sugars **5.6g**; Protein **8.6g**

Gandhi Bowl

Serves 2 | "Be the change you want to see in the world." —Gandhi

1 medium russet potato, diced
1 tsp mild curry powder, divided
salt, to taste
pepper, to taste
1 10-oz package frozen greens
1 15-oz can chickpeas, drained and rinsed
2 tbsp tomato paste
½ tsp granulated onion powder
½ tsp granulated garlic powder
½ tsp ground cumin
½ tsp chili powder, or to taste
¼ tsp ground ginger

1. Preheat oven to 400°F. Grease cookie sheet and set aside.
2. Transfer potato to a mixing bowl and spray with cooking spray.
3. Sprinkle ½ tsp of curry powder over top with salt and pepper.
4. Mix to coat.
5. Re-spray and mix again.
6. Place potatoes in a single layer on the cookie sheet and bake for 7 to 15 minutes, or until cooked and crisp.
7. Meanwhile, cook greens according to package instructions, squeezing out any excess water, and set aside.
8. Transfer chickpeas to a nonstick skillet.
9. In a 1-cup glass/liquid measuring cup, add tomato paste and remaining seasonings, plus salt and pepper to taste.
10. Add water until it's filled to the 1-cup mark.
11. Whisk to combine.
12. Pour mixture over chickpeas, then stir to coat.
13. Cook over high heat until the liquid has evaporated, about 12 minutes, stirring every minute or so.
14. Make a bed of greens, then add chickpeas in the center with potatoes on each side.

NUTRITIONAL INFORMATION 🥄 Calories **348**; Calories from Fat **23**; Total Fat **2.5g**; Cholesterol **0mg**; Total Carbohydrate **65.8g**; Dietary Fiber **14.5g**; Sugars **5.4g**; Protein **18.6g**

Lasagna Rolls

Serves 4 | When I was in law school, I used to make a big batch of vegetable lasagna right before final exams. I'd freeze individual portions and then reheat a serving each night for a warm and comforting meal. I still like to cook up a big batch and keep leftovers in the freezer, only now I make lasagna rolls, which make single servings even easier.

1 8-oz box whole-wheat or brown rice lasagna noodles
1 10-oz package frozen spinach, thawed
1 recipe Tofu Ricotta Cheese (pg. 266)
¼ c vegan Parmesan
salt, to taste
nutritional yeast, to taste
Italian seasoning, to taste
pepper, to taste
1 25-oz jar marinara sauce

1. In a large pot of salted water, cook pasta al dente, according to package directions.
2. Immediately rinse with cold water, pat dry with a clean towel, and set aside, laying flat on a plate.
3. Press out any excess water from spinach and combine with Tofu Ricotta Cheese and vegan Parmesan in a large bowl until well incorporated.
4. Once evenly combined, taste, adding salt as desired and adjusting nutritional yeast, Parmesan, and other seasonings, such as Italian seasoning or pepper.
5. Then add ½ cup of marinara and stir to combine.
6. Line your large pot with a thin layer of marinara.
7. On a clean work surface, spread ¼ cup of the tofu-spinach mixture on a noodle and roll it closed.
8. Place the roll in the pot with the crease facing down.
9. Repeat with all noodles.
10. Pour the remaining marinara over the rolls, cover, and bring to a boil.
11. Once boiling, reduce heat to medium and simmer for about 5 minutes, until rolls and marinara are warm.
12. Serve immediately.

NUTRITIONAL INFORMATION 👓 Calories **420**; Calories from Fat **65.8**; Total Fat **7.3g**; Cholesterol **0mg**; Total Carbohydrate **65.9g**; Dietary Fiber **9.2g**; Sugars **1g**; Protein **25.4g**

Hawaiian Chickpea Teriyaki

Serves 2 | *Pictured opposite* | This is my vegan spin on Hawaiian barbecue. In Hawaii, meats are commonly marinated in teriyaki sauce before grilling and, lucky for us, the salty and spicy teriyaki also goes perfectly with the nutty flavor of chickpeas. Plus the fresh sweetness of the pineapple salsa adds another dimension you just can't beat.

1 15-oz can chickpeas, drained and rinsed
¼ c teriyaki sauce
1 tbsp Szechuan sauce or hot sauce (optional)
1 tbsp raw sugar (optional)
2 c cooked brown rice (or cooked greens)
pineapple and/or mango salsa (see Chef's Note)

1. Combine chickpeas, teriyaki sauce, Szechuan sauce, and sugar in a large frying pan.

2. Allow to marinate for at least 5 minutes.

3. Cook over medium heat, stirring regularly, until most of the liquid has absorbed, about 10 minutes.

4. Spoon over cooked rice and top with salsa. (For a lighter dish, you can substitute cooked greens, such as steamed kale, for the rice.)

CHEF'S NOTE: *If you want to create your own pineapple and mango salsa, mix equal parts chopped pineapple and mango with minced red onion, fresh cilantro, and lime juice to taste.*

NUTRITIONAL INFORMATION 🍲 Calories **505**; Calories from Fat **30**; Total Fat **3.4g**; Cholesterol **0mg**; Total Carbohydrate **99.4g**; Dietary Fiber **12.8g**; Sugars **15.0g**; Protein **19.1g**

Maque Choux

Serves 2 | Maque Choux (pronounced "mock shoe") is traditionally served as an accompaniment in Creole cuisine, but I think it makes a wonderful meal on its own when paired with rice and kidney beans or sliced Spicy Sausage (pg. 150).

1 small onion, finely diced
4 garlic cloves, minced
1 green bell pepper, seeded and finely diced
1 to 2 tsp Cajun Essence (pg. 274)
2 celery stalks, finely diced (optional)
1 15-oz can fire-roasted diced tomatoes, drained
2 c frozen yellow corn
salt, to taste
pepper, to taste
hot sauce, to taste
1 c cooked brown rice
1 c kidney beans or sliced Spicy Sausage (pg. 150)

1. Line a medium saucepan with a thin layer of water or broth.

2. Cook onion over high heat. Once translucent, add garlic, bell pepper, Cajun Essence, and celery.

3. Continue to cook, adding more water or broth as necessary, until bell peppers are bright green and cooked but still very crisp.

4. Add tomatoes and corn, reduce heat to medium, and heat thoroughly. Add salt, pepper, and hot sauce if desired.

5. Serve over a bed of cooked brown rice and toss with kidney beans or Spicy Sausage.

NUTRITIONAL INFORMATION 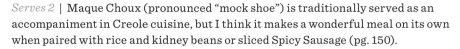 Calories **215**; Calories from Fat **23**; Total Fat **2.5g**; Cholesterol **0mg**; Total Carbohydrate **47.0g**; Dietary Fiber **9.0g**; Sugars **14.9g**; Protein **8.3g**

Tofu Chilaquiles

Serves 4 | Tofu Chilaquiles is my favorite dish to order at Swingers in Los Angeles. It's traditionally served at brunch, but I like it best as a quick dinner in the summer when tomatoes and corn are at their peak.

1 onion, diced
4 garlic cloves, minced
½ tsp chili powder
2 tsp ground cumin
1 lb extra-firm tofu, drained
   and pressed
1 12-oz jar salsa verde
1 c cooked or canned
   black beans
2 c frozen yellow corn,
   thawed
2 c diced tomatoes or
   chunky salsa
baked corn chips
fresh cilantro (optional)

1. Line a large skillet with a thin layer of water.
2. Add onion, garlic, and spices. Cook over high heat until onion is translucent, about 4 minutes.
3. Add tofu and salsa verde.
4. Use a spatula to break the tofu into pieces.
5. Stir to evenly incorporate all ingredients.
6. Continue to cook, stirring every so often, until most of the liquid has been absorbed, about 10 minutes.
7. Stir in black beans, reduce heat to medium, and continue to cook until black beans are warm and liquid has evaporated.
8. Stir in corn.
9. Spoon into serving bowls and add tomatoes.
10. Crumble corn chips over top and garnish with fresh cilantro.

> **CHEF'S NOTE:** *Serve with extra corn chips and hot sauce on the table.*

NUTRITIONAL INFORMATION 🍲 Calories **164**; Calories from Fat **22**; Total Fat **2.4g**; Cholesterol **0mg**; Total Carbohydrate **26.6g**; Dietary Fiber **4.1g**; Sugars **7.5g**; Protein **12.9g**

Mexican Cabbage

Serves 2 | *Pictured opposite* | This recipe is just dying to prove to you that cabbage is not bland! It's spicy, flavorful, and a little sassy.

1 small sweet onion,
  chopped
2 garlic cloves, minced
½ medium head of cabbage,
  chopped into thin strips
1 8-oz can tomato sauce
1 4-oz can green chilies,
  minced
2 tbsp tomato paste
1 tsp ground cumin
½ tsp oregano or marjoram
1 c frozen yellow corn
salt, to taste
pepper, to taste
1 c cooked or canned
  black beans
baked corn tortilla chips

1. Line a medium saucepan with water and cook onion and garlic over high heat until translucent.

2. Add cabbage, tomato sauce, chilies, tomato paste, and spices.

3. Reduce heat to medium and cook until cabbage is tender, about 10 minutes.

4. Turn off heat and stir in corn until evenly distributed.

5. Taste, adjusting spices as needed. Add salt and pepper if desired.

6. Mix in black beans before serving.

7. Break corn tortilla chips into small pieces in your hand and sprinkle over top before serving.

NUTRITIONAL INFORMATION 🥄 Calories **294**; Calories from Fat **24**; Total Fat **2.7g**; Cholesterol **0mg**; Total Carbohydrate **59.0g**; Dietary Fiber **17.7g**; Sugars **16.5g**; Protein **14.8g**

Seitan Pot Roast

Serves 4 | *Pictured opposite* | Just like Mom used to make, only better. Serve with No-Beef Gravy (pg. 254) and fresh bread. Leftover pot roast slices are also great in sandwiches.

1 c vital wheat gluten

2 tsp granulated onion powder

1 tsp granulated garlic powder

1 tsp dried thyme

⅛ tsp pepper

2 tbsp Vegan Worcestershire Sauce (pg. 272)

3 to 4 c No-Beef Broth (pg. 279), divided

1 yellow onion, thinly sliced

4 garlic cloves, minced

2 medium russet potatoes, chopped

4 large carrots, peeled and chopped

salt, to taste

pepper, to taste

> **CHEF'S NOTE:**
> *Serve with vegetables and spoon excess juices over top.*

1. In a large bowl, whisk vital wheat gluten with spices until well combined. Add Vegan Worcestershire Sauce and 1 cup of No-Beef Broth and stir. Dough should form instantly.

2. Knead dough (seitan) in the bowl for about a minute to remove any bubbles.

3. Give the dough a good squeeze so it releases any extra water and set aside. Dough should be in the shape of a ball of dough, but don't fuss about the shape; any somewhat round mass will do.

4. Line the center of a large pot with onion and garlic, lightly seasoning them with salt and pepper. Place the seitan on top of the onion then surround the seitan with potatoes and carrots, lightly seasoning them with salt and pepper. Pour any leftover cooking liquid over top.

5. Pour 2 cups of broth over the seitan and vegetables, adding more if necessary. The seitan and vegetables should be sitting in broth (it's better to have too much than too little).

6. Cover and cook over low heat for 1 hour or until the vegetables are tender and seitan has expanded.

7. Meanwhile, preheat your oven to 350°F. Grease a cookie sheet and set aside. Once seitan and vegetables are cooked, bake seitan on the cookie sheet for 20 to 25 minutes, or until the outside is firm and lightly browned.

NUTRITIONAL INFORMATION (WITH VEGETABLES; WITHOUT GRAVY)
Calories **257**; Calories from Fat 8; Total Fat **0.8g**; Cholesterol **0mg**; Total Carbohydrate **37.7g**; Dietary Fiber **5.2g**; Sugars **6.9g**; Protein **26.1g**

Tofu & Vegan Meats

Bacon Bits

Makes 1 cup | *Pictured opposite* | Bacon Bits and other similar brands at the grocery store are usually accidentally vegan. However, they often have corn syrup, hydrogenated oils, food colorings, and weird preservatives that aren't so healthy. Here is a quick and easy recipe to make them at home. Sprinkle over salads, Baked Shells and Cheese (pg. 156), or with Herbed Home Fries (pg. 30).

2 tbsp soy sauce
1½ tsp liquid smoke
2 tsp pure maple syrup
¼ tsp granulated garlic
   powder
⅛ tsp paprika
½ c TVP or TSP
salt, as needed

1. Combine soy sauce, liquid smoke, 1 tbsp of water, maple syrup, garlic powder, and paprika in a small saucepan and bring to a boil.

2. Once it's boiling, immediately turn off the heat and stir in TVP or TSP.

3. Continue to stir until all the liquid has been absorbed.

4. Add salt as needed.

5. Next you'll need to crisp up and dehydrate the bits. You can either set your toaster oven to 200°F and toast the crumbs, shaking the tray every 2 minutes to prevent burning and repeating until crisp, or fry in a nonstick pan until crispy, stirring often.

NUTRITIONAL INFORMATION ✎ Calories **27**; Calories from Fat **0**; Total Fat **0.0g**; Cholesterol **0mg**; Total Carbohydrate **3.3g**; Dietary Fiber **1.1g**; Sugars **1.8g**; Protein **3.3g**

Basic Baked Tofu

Makes 8 cutlets | Baking tofu changes the texture—it becomes chewy and meaty and a blank canvas for just about any sauce. I like to smother baked tofu in Cranberry Sauce (pg. 267) or Southern-Style BBQ Sauce (pg. 256) and slap it into a sandwich with lettuce, tomatoes, and mustard. Super Protein tofu is my favorite tofu to use here, but extra-firm tofu is a fine substitution and more readily available.

1 lb extra-firm tofu

1. Preheat oven to 350°F. Line baking sheet with parchment paper and set aside.

2. Cut tofu into 8 to 10 strips and transfer to cookie sheet.

3. Bake for 8 minutes. Flip and bake for another 8 minutes, or until the tofu is golden brown and slightly crisp on the outside but tender on the inside. If you prefer a softer texture or are pressed for time, you can skip the second baking.

VARIATION

Marinated Tofu ⬤ Ⓕ Ⓖ 😊 ✎ Brush the front and back of tofu slices with soy sauce, Italian dressing, or any other marinade and let marinate for 30 minutes before baking.

> **CHEF'S NOTE:** *For a larger cutlet, you can alternatively cut 4¼-inch strips and bake for 30 minutes.*

NUTRITIONAL INFORMATION PER PIECE ✎ Calories **20.6**; Calories from Fat **3.1**; Total Fat **0.3g**; Cholesterol **0mg**; Total Carbohydrate **0.7g**; Dietary Fiber **0g**; Sugars **0g**; Protein **3.4g**

Baked Tofu Parmesan

Serves 4 | Like any good Italian, I love my pasta, but sometimes I want something a little heartier. Since I'm not a fan of eggplant, one day I substituted tofu in a Parmesan recipe. I've been in my blue tofu heaven ever since.

1 lb Super Protein tofu or extra-firm tofu, pressed
1 c Breadcrumbs (pg. 284)
4 tbsp vegan Parmesan
2 tbsp Italian seasoning
¼ tsp fine salt
⅛ tsp pepper
½ non-dairy milk
1 tbsp cornstarch
1 28-oz jar marinara sauce

CHEF'S NOTE:
Working with ¼ cup of the breadcrumb mixture at a time prevents the breading from becoming too wet. If the breading becomes too moist, it won't stick to the tofu.

1. Preheat oven to 350°F. Line a cookie sheet with parchment paper and set aside.
2. Turn tofu on its side and cut 12 evenly sized cutlets; set aside.
3. Combine Breadcrumbs, Parmesan, spices, salt, and pepper, then finely grind in a food processor or mortar and pestle to a fine, sand-like consistency.
4. Pour crumb mixture into a shallow bowl.
5. Whisk non-dairy milk and cornstarch together, then pour into another shallow bowl.
6. Dip each tofu cutlet into the non-dairy milk mixture, briefly submerging it, then immediately into the Breadcrumbs.
7. Flip the tofu over and press into the Breadcrumbs again, repeating as necessary until the cutlet is well coated.
8. Repeat with remaining cutlets, placing the finished product on the cookie sheet.
9. Spray with cooking spray and bake for 12 minutes.
10. Flip and re-spray, baking for 10 minutes more.
11. Arrange cutlets on a plate and cover with marinara and garnish with vegan Parmesan.

NUTRITIONAL INFORMATION (PER SERVING: 3 CUTLETS) Calories **274**; Calories from Fat **49**; Total Fat **5.5g**; Cholesterol **0mg**; Total Carbohydrate **38.1g**; Dietary Fiber **3.8g**; Sugars **22.0g**; Protein **18.8g**

Breakfast Sausage Patties

Makes 16 patties | *Pictured on pg. 21* | Quinoa and maple transform Gimme Lean into the perfect breakfast sausage. It has a nice, firm texture with a hint of smoke and sweetness from the maple syrup.

1 c cooked quinoa
1 14-oz tube Gimme Lean
   Sausage Style
2 tbsp pure maple syrup
¼ tsp liquid smoke
   (optional)

1. Make sure quinoa is cool to the touch.
2. With wet hands, mix the ingredients until well combined, using additional maple syrup if you prefer a sweeter sausage.
3. Break off walnut-size pieces, roll into a ball, and then flatten with your palms.
4. Repeat until you have 12 to 16 patties.
5. Heat a nonstick pan or greased skillet over medium heat and pan-fry, flipping every minute or so, until well cooked and slightly brown on each side, about 8 to 12 minutes total.

TVP Beef Crumbles

Makes 2 cups (serves 4) | Use these crumbles the way you'd use ground chuck. Add them to marinara sauce, pizza sauce, casseroles, vegetable lasagna, or chili.

1 c No-Beef Broth (pg. 279)
1 c TVP
1 tbsp Vegan Worcestershire
   Sauce (pg. 272)
4 tsp steak sauce

1. Bring No-Beef Broth to a boil. Combine broth and TVP. Once reconstituted, stir in remaining ingredients.

NUTRITIONAL INFORMATION

BREAKFAST SAUSAGE PATTIES Calories **82**; Calories from Fat **4**; Total Fat **0.2g**; Cholesterol **0mg**; Total Carbohydrate **11.4g**; Dietary Fiber **2.2g**; Sugars **3.8g**; Protein **8.0g**

TVP BEEF CRUMBLES Calories **90**; Calories from Fat **0**; Total Fat **0.0g**; Cholesterol **0mg**; Total Carbohydrate **9.5g**; Dietary Fiber **4.0g**; Sugars **4.4g**; Protein **12.1g**

Cajun Meatloaf ✪

Serves 4 | This "meatloaf" is made with Cajun spicing and the holy trinity: celery, bell peppers, and onions. You can make the loaf as spicy as you prefer by using hot sauce instead of water. Serve with Spicy Greens (pg. 184), Cornbread (pg. 49), Creole Roasted Red-Pepper Sauce (pg. 257), or ketchup.

1 red bell pepper, seeded and minced
1 small onion, minced
2 celery stalks, rinsed and minced
3 garlic cloves, minced
1 14-oz package Gimme Lean Beef Style
3 tbsp steak sauce or ketchup
2 tbsp prepared yellow mustard
1 tbsp Vegan Worcestershire Sauce (pg. 272)
1 tbsp Cajun Essence
¼ c water or hot sauce, or a combination
1 c Breadcrumbs (pg. 284)

1. Preheat oven to 350°F. Grease a standard 8-inch loaf pan and set aside.

2. Place bell pepper, onion, celery, and garlic in a food processor one at a time, pulsing until they're finely chopped but not completely minced or pureed.

3. Transfer each ingredient to a large mixing bowl after it has been shredded.

4. Add remaining ingredients to the mixing bowl and thoroughly combine, using your hands or a spatula.

5. Transfer to a loaf pan and pat down firmly with a spatula.

6. Grab a large sheet of aluminum foil and make a tent over the top of the loaf.

7. Bake for 1 hour, then uncover and bake an additional 10 to 30 minutes, until the outside is brown and firm and the inside is not loose.

8. Cool in the pan for 10 to 20 minutes before serving, allowing the meatloaf to firm up a bit for easy slicing.

> **CHEF'S NOTE:** *Allow the Gimme Lean to sit out for 30 minutes to 1 hour, if possible, so it is easier to work with.*

NUTRITIONAL INFORMATION (PER SERVING: APPROX. 2 SLICES)
Calories **193**; Calories from Fat **13**; Total Fat **1.4g**; Cholesterol **0mg**; Total Carbohydrate **26.2g**; Dietary Fiber **6.8g**; Sugars **8.1g**; Protein **18.8g**

Chicken-Style Seitan Ⓕ Ⓢ 😃

Serves 4 | A dead ringer for country-fried or baked chicken, this seitan is easy to make and incredibly versatile. A crisp outer "skin" forms during baking while the inside stays tender and juicy.

½ c vital wheat gluten
1½ tsp No-Chicken
   Broth Powder
   (pg. 281; optional)
2 c No-Chicken Broth
   (pg. 281)
¼ c nutritional yeast
1½ tsp Poultry Seasoning
   Mix (pg. 273)
1 tsp granulated onion
   powder
salt, to taste
pepper, to taste

CHEF'S NOTE: *If using a commercial bouillon cube or regular vegetable broth, only use 1 cup and substitute water for the other cup or your seitan may be too salty.*

1. In a mixing bowl, combine vital wheat gluten, No-Chicken Broth Powder, and ½ cup of warm water, stirring until a dough forms.

2. Turn dough (seitan) out onto a clean surface and knead for 1 minute, then set aside.

3. Combine 2 cups of broth with nutritional yeast and seasonings in a large pot, stirring to incorporate.

4. Return to dough and cut into strips, breasts, or any other shape, being mindful that it will more than double in size during cooking.

5. Bring broth to a boil and add dough.

6. Bring to a boil again, then reduce heat to low and simmer with the lid slightly ajar for 50 minutes to 1 hour, stirring every 10 to 15 minutes. Save any excess liquid left in the pot.

7. Preheat oven to 350°F. Meanwhile, grease a large casserole dish or cookie sheet that is large enough to fit all of your pieces without them having to touch.

8. Once dough is finished cooking, bake for 20 to 30 minutes, until a golden skin has formed.

9. Flip over halfway through cooking if desired.

10. To make a gravy, add up to 1 cup of non-dairy milk to the leftover cooking liquid then heat over medium heat, adding salt and pepper as desired.

NUTRITIONAL INFORMATION 🥄 Calories 85; Calories from Fat 4; Total Fat **0.4g**; Cholesterol **0mg**; Total Carbohydrate **7.6g**; Dietary Fiber **0.8g**; Sugars **0.7g**; Protein **13.1g**

Hippie Loaf Ⓖ 😊

Serves 4 | *Pictured on pg. 134* | My friend Talia has celiac disease and solicited my help in creating a gluten-free veggie meatloaf recipe. We started trading ideas about how to make a meatloaf out of the items in our pantry, and this is what we came up with. It's absolutely delicious and one of the most popular recipes on my website, Happyherbivore.com. Serve with Dirty Mashed Potatoes (pg. 190), Brown Gravy (pg. 254), Maple-Glazed Vegetables (pg. 174), and steamed green beans.

1 15-oz can black beans, drained and rinsed
1 onion, diced
2 garlic cloves, minced
1 large carrot, peeled and shredded
2 celery stalks, washed and shredded
1 c coarsely chopped brown mushrooms
1 c cooked quinoa
1 tbsp Italian seasoning
3 tbsp brown rice flour
2 tbsp soy sauce
2 tbsp ketchup

1. Preheat oven to 350°F.
2. Grease a standard 8-inch loaf pan and set aside.
3. Mash black beans in a large bowl and combine all ingredients until evenly combined.
4. Transfer to prepared pan and pat down firmly and tightly using a spatula.
5. Bake for 45 minutes to 1 hour, until firm and brown on the outside.
6. Allow the loaf to cool and firm up before serving, about 15 to 20 minutes.

> **CHEF'S NOTE:** *Whole-wheat flour may be substituted for brown rice flour.*

NUTRITIONAL INFORMATION (PER SERVING: APPROX. 2 SLICES) 🐘
Calories **190**; Calories from Fat **17**; Total Fat **1.9g**; Cholesterol **0mg**; Total Carbohydrate **34.1g**; Dietary Fiber **7.5g**; Sugars **4.3g**; Protein **9.7g**

Seitan Piccata

Serves 4 | This is a healthy and vegan version of the classic Italian dish. Serve with steamed asparagus and a starch such as rice or pasta.

1 recipe Chicken-Style
   Seitan (pg. 142)
2 tbsp cornstarch
1 onion, finely diced
3 garlic cloves, minced
1 tbsp capers, drained
1 tbsp Poultry Seasoning
   Mix (pg. 273)
1 tsp dried parsley
1 c white wine
2 tbsp fresh lemon juice
pinch of lemon zest
salt, to taste
pepper, to taste

1. Prepare the Chicken-Style Seitan, cutting the dough into 4 thin cutlets.

2. Mix cornstarch with 2 tbsp of water and set aside.

3. Line a medium saucepan with a thin layer of water.

4. Cook onion and garlic over high heat until onion is translucent, about 3 minutes.

5. Add capers, Poultry Seasoning Mix, and parsley and cook for 2 minutes more.

6. Add wine and lemon juice and cook until the liquid reduces by half.

7. Add 1 cup of water and lemon zest and cook until liquid reduces by half again.

8. Taste, adding more lemon juice if desired.

9. Add cornstarch mixture, reduce heat to medium, and allow the sauce to slightly thicken.

10. Salt and pepper to taste, then serve over Chicken-Style Seitan.

NUTRITIONAL INFORMATION ⟶ Calories **169**; Calories from Fat **5**; Total Fat **0.6g**; Cholesterol **0mg**; Total Carbohydrate **17.6g**; Dietary Fiber **1.6g**; Sugars **2.6g**; Protein **13.8g**

Mexican Chorizo

Serves 3 | *Pictured opposite* | Chorizo is a spicy pork sausage originating from the Iberian peninsula, but it has deep roots in Mexican cuisine as well. After I came across a commercial soy version in Los Angeles, I set out to make my own. Because the flavor comes from the spices and not the meat itself, it's an easy dish to replicate—and really tasty! Serve with Tofu Scramble (pg. 18), Spicy Greens (pg. 184), Cornbread (pg. 49), or TVP Tacos (pg. 98).

1 tbsp red wine vinegar
2 tbsp soy sauce or tamari
1 tsp granulated garlic powder
1¼ tsp granulated onion powder
1 tsp paprika
1 tsp oregano or marjoram
1 tsp ground cumin
1 tbsp chili powder
dash or two of ground cinnamon
3 tbsp ketchup
1 tbsp prepared yellow mustard
1 c TVP or quinoa
⅛ tsp liquid smoke (optional)
hot sauce, to taste
salt, to taste
pepper, to taste

1. Whisk 2 cups of water with red wine vinegar, soy sauce, garlic powder, onion powder, paprika, oregano or marjoram, cumin, chili powder, cinnamon, ketchup, and mustard together until well combined.

2. Add TVP or quinoa, cover and bring to a boil. Once boiling, reduce heat to medium and continue to cook, stirring every so often, until all the water has absorbed, about 10 to 20 minutes.

3. Add liquid smoke if using, then salt, pepper, and hot sauce, stirring to combine.

4. Set aside, covered, for 15 to 30 minutes to allow flavors to merge before serving.

CHEF'S NOTE: *If the liquid has not cooked off after 20 minutes, remove lid and cook uncovered.*

NUTRITIONAL INFORMATION 🍽 Calories **151**; Calories from Fat **9**; Total Fat **0.9g**; Cholesterol **0mg**; Total Carbohydrate **18.0g**; Dietary Fiber **7.1g**; Sugars **8.5g**; Protein **18.0g**

Portobello Steaks

Makes 2 | *Pictured opposite* | These portobellos are juicy and tender and make a great vegan substitute for steak. Serve them whole with a baked potato and side of vegetables or slice them up thickly for Steak and Pepper Fajitas (pg. 103). Serve with green beans or mixed vegetables and a Twice-Baked Potato (pg. 191) or Dijon Mashed Potatoes (pg. 190).

1 tsp dried thyme
1 tsp dried chives
½ tsp dried basil
¼ to 1 c No-Beef Broth
   (pg. 279) or water
½ small onion, minced
1 garlic clove, minced
3 tbsp balsamic vinegar
1 tbsp sherry or mirin
2 portobello mushrooms,
   stems removed
salt, to taste

1. Grind herbs to a fine consistency using mortar and pestle.

2. Line a large frying pan with a thin layer of No-Beef Broth or water.

3. Cook onion and garlic over high heat for about 2 minutes.

4. Once the liquid starts to boil, add vinegar, sherry or mirin, and ground spices.

5. Reduce heat to medium, add another ¼ cup of broth or water, and bring to a boil.

6. Add mushrooms and cook for 5 minutes.

7. Gently flip mushrooms over and cook for another 5 minutes, adding more water or broth as necessary. Repeat if necessary, cooking until mushrooms are soft and tender.

8. Remove from heat and plate.

9. Sprinkle a little salt over top and drizzle with leftover juices.

NUTRITIONAL INFORMATION 🥄 Calories **51**; Calories from Fat **3**; Total Fat **0.3g**; Cholesterol **0mg**; Total Carbohydrate **8.6g**; Dietary Fiber **2.2g**; Sugars **3.0g**; Protein **3.2g**

Spicy Sausage ★

Makes 4 sausages | *Pictured opposite* | This sausage is a cross between andouille sausage and pepperoni. It's great for nibbling, sliced on top of pizza, crumbled into a Frittata (pg. 15) and Baked Shells and Cheese (pg. 156), or tossed with a batch of Spicy Greens (pg. 184).

½ c cooked or canned pinto
  beans
1 tbsp fennel seeds
1 tbsp cayenne powder
1 tsp rubbed sage (not
  powdered)
1 tsp red pepper flakes
1 tsp granulated garlic
  powder
1 tsp granulated onion
  powder
¼ tsp chili powder
¼ tsp dried thyme
¼ c TVP
¾ c vital wheat gluten
¼ c nutritional yeast
2 tbsp soy sauce
2 tsp hot sauce

1. Pulse pinto beans in a food processor until they're coarse crumbs or mash with a fork; set aside.

2. Grind fennel seeds using a mortar and pestle into a thin powder, then combine with all other spices.

3. Transfer beans and spices to a medium bowl. Add remaining ingredients in order plus 1 cup of water.

4. Stir a few times, then combine ingredients with your hands.

5. Knead for a minute or two to ensure even distribution and to help push the bubbles out (under-kneading may cause a spongy texture).

6. Shape mixture into a ball and break into 4 even segments and set aside.

7. Shape each segment into a log—do not worry about molding sausages perfectly; the steaming process will help shape them.

8. Prepare 4 sheets of aluminum foil, each about 5 inches square. Wrap dough in foil tightly and twist both ends so it looks like a Tootsie Roll.

9. Place sausages into a steamer, cover, and cook for 40 minutes.

10. Refrigerate overnight or for at least 4 hours.

11. To use, warm gently in oven or toaster oven for 8 to 10 minutes.

NUTRITIONAL INFORMATION (SERVING: 1 SAUSAGE) ⬅ Calories **169**;
Calories from Fat **12**; Total Fat **1.4g**; Cholesterol **0mg**; Total Carbohydrate **15.6g**; Dietary Fiber **4.6g**;
Sugars **1.7g**; Protein **24.4g**

Torkey (Tofu Turkey)

Makes 5 breasts | I have always loved cooking a big Thanksgiving meal, and going vegan didn't change that. In fact I'd wager to say I find cooking a vegan Thanksgiving a thousand times more enjoyable. Serve this tofu turkey with Dirty Mashed Potatoes (pg. 190), Thanksgiving Gravy (pg. 255), Traditional Stuffing (pg. 195), Cranberry Sauce (pg. 267), green beans, and Pumpkin Pie (pg. 218).

14 oz Super Protein or
    extra-firm tofu
1 small onion
1 small parsnip, peeled
1 c rolled oats
2 to 3 tbsp Poultry
    Seasoning Mix (pg. 273)
2 tbsp yellow miso paste
¼ tsp pepper
2 tbsp vegetarian chicken
    broth powder (optional)

1. If using extra-firm tofu, press for 20 minutes, than place in a Ziploc bag and freeze overnight. Let tofu completely thaw before using.

2. If you have a food processor, attach the shredding blade and shred the tofu, then transfer tofu to a large mixing bowl. Otherwise, run the tofu along a cheese grater, letting the long strands fall into a mixing bowl.

3. Shred onion and parsnip using a food processor; alternatively, mince both by hand.

4. Using your hands, combine all ingredients together in a large mixing bowl.

5. Mix for at least a few minutes, particularly if you manually shredded the tofu. You want the mixture to be very crumbly, almost like cottage cheese.

6. Set aside and preheat oven to 350°F.

7. Lightly grease a cookie sheet or line it with parchment paper.

8. Using a wide ½-cup measuring cup, pack mixture down firmly, then transfer mold onto the cookie sheet.

9. Repeat until you have 5 patties.

10. Spray with oil or cooking spray and bake for 25 to 35 minutes, until the outside is golden brown and crisp.

NUTRITIONAL INFORMATION (PER SERVING: 1 "BREAST") Calories **117**; Calories from Fat **19**; Total Fat **2.1g**; Cholesterol **0mg**; Total Carbohydrate **16.3g**; Dietary Fiber **2.6g**; Sugars **1.8g**; Protein **8.8g**

Veggie, Bean, & Quinoa Croquettes

Serves 4 | Ask me for a food that transcends all cultures and I'll hand you a croquette. Known by many other names, croquettes are served worldwide and are commonly made of meat, potatoes, vegetables, or a combination thereof. We have croquettes here in the United States, too, except we know them colloquially as crab cakes. Unlike their traditional cousins, these croquettes are baked instead of fried and are made from beans, veggies, and quinoa.

1 15-oz can kidney beans, drained
1 small onion, minced
1 medium zucchini, minced
1 large carrot, peeled and minced
2 garlic cloves, minced
1 c cooked quinoa
2 tbsp low-sodium soy sauce
2 tbsp ketchup
2 tbsp steak sauce
1 tbsp prepared yellow mustard
1 tbsp Italian seasoning
¼ c vital wheat gluten
½ c Breadcrumbs (pg. 284)
Creole Roasted Red-Pepper Sauce (pg. 257) or your favorite marinara (optional)

1. Preheat oven to 350°F.
2. Grease a cookie sheet or line it with parchment paper and set aside.
3. In a large bowl, mash kidney beans.
4. Combine the beans with all remaining ingredients except Breadcrumbs until evenly combined.
5. Using your hands, mold mixture into walnut-sized balls and roll gently in Breadcrumbs.
6. Place on cookie sheet.
7. Bake for 25 to 30 minutes, or until lightly brown and a firm outer crust forms.
8. Set aside for 10 to 15 minutes before serving, allowing the balls to cool and firm up.
9. Serve with Creole Roasted Red-Pepper Sauce (or your favorite marinara) poured over top.

> **CHEF'S NOTE:** *To use this recipe for making meatballs for the Meatball Sub (pg. 109), omit the Breadcrumbs and shape the mixture into larger, round balls.*

NUTRITIONAL INFORMATION 🍶 Calories **140**; Calories from Fat **8**; Total Fat **0.9g**; Cholesterol **0mg**; Total Carbohydrate **23.7g**; Dietary Fiber **7.2g**; Sugars **4.6g**; Protein **10.8g**

Pasta & Casseroles

Baked Shells and Cheese

Serves 4 | *Pictured opposite* | Mac 'n' cheese is an all-American favorite, but our friends down South do it right by baking it. A thin, cheesy crust is the perfect complement to rich and creamy mac 'n' cheese. I use shell-shaped pasta.

½ lb uncooked whole-wheat or brown rice pasta
1¼ c non-dairy milk
½ c nutritional yeast
2 tbsp yellow miso
1 tsp prepared yellow mustard
1 tbsp onion flakes
1 tsp granulated garlic powder
½ tsp paprika
¼ tsp turmeric
1 12.3-oz package firm Mori-Nu tofu, drained
Breadcrumbs (pg. 284; optional)
vegan Parmesan (optional)
salt, to taste
pepper, to taste

1. Preheat oven to 350°F.
2. Cook pasta al dente according to package directions and immediately rinse with cold water.
3. In a medium saucepan, whisk non-dairy milk, nutritional yeast, miso, mustard, and spices together and bring to a boil over medium-high heat.
4. Meanwhile, combine tofu with 2 tbsp of water in a blender and puree until smooth and set aside.
5. Once the non-dairy milk mixture is boiling, remove from heat and add in cooked pasta and tofu, stirring to coat evenly.
6. Add salt and pepper and stir again.
7. Transfer to an oven-safe square casserole dish.
8. Top with Breadcrumbs or vegan Parmesan if desired and bake for 20 to 25 minutes, or until the top is slightly browned.

VARIATIONS

Tex-Mex Chili Stir in 1 15-oz can of vegetarian chili.

Broccoli Casserole Stir in 2 cups of cooked, but still crisp, fresh, or frozen broccoli florets.

Cheeseburger Mac Stir in 4 crumbled vegan burger patties.

NUTRITIONAL INFORMATION Calories **326**; Calories from Fat **34**; Total Fat **3.8g**; Cholesterol **0mg**; Total Carbohydrate **52.8g**; Dietary Fiber **7.7g**; Sugars **5.6g**; Protein **21.2g**

Easy Macaroni and Cheese

Serves 2 | *Pictured opposite* | A quick, easy, and healthy vegan alternative to commercial mac 'n' cheeses.

1¼ c uncooked brown
   rice macaroni
Cheddar Cheesy Sauce
   (pg. 264)
1 tbsp cornstarch
salt, to taste
pepper, to taste
smoked paprika (optional)

1. Cook pasta according to package directions.

2. Immediately drain pasta, rinse with cold water, and set aside.

3. Whisk the ingredients for the Cheddar Cheesy Sauce together with an additional 1 tbsp of cornstarch in a saucepan, plus add salt and pepper.

4. Bring to a near boil over medium heat then reduce heat to low.

5. Continue to cook, stirring occasionally, until the sauce thickens.

6. Combine sauce with cooked pasta, stirring to coat, and heat thoroughly.

7. Garnish with a light dusting of smoked paprika before serving.

CHEF'S NOTE: *If you want an even thicker sauce, add another 1 tbs cornstarch mixed into 1 to 2 tbsp of water.*

NUTRITIONAL INFORMATION 🐟 Calories **324**; Calories from Fat **36**; Total Fat **3.9g**; Saturated Fat **0.6g**; Cholesterol **0mg**; Total Carbohydrate **56.6g**; Dietary Fiber **8.2g**; Sugars **6.5g**; Protein **16.0g**

Broccoli Pesto Pasta

Serves 2 | *Pictured opposite* | This northern Italian dish is traditionally made with basil and pine nuts, but parsley, almonds, and oil are sometimes used as a substitution or variation. I've taken the nuts out in this version, but you'll still find it as decadent and satisfying as the original pesto. The addition of broccoli also adds a rustic dimension to the pesto and enhances the overall nutrition of the dish. Corkscrew-shaped pastas such as rotini work best here, as the twists help hold the sauce, but feel free to use any pasta you like. Sliced or cherry tomatoes, pitted kalamata olives, and roasted red pepper slices are nice additions to this dish.

3 c fresh broccoli florets
½ to 1 c fresh basil leaves, packed tight
3 garlic cloves
1 to 2 tbsp lemon juice
4 to 5 tbsp vegan Parmesan or nutritional yeast
½ c silken tofu
salt, to taste
pepper, to taste
8 oz uncooked whole-wheat or brown rice pasta
¼ c marinara (optional)

CHEF'S NOTE:
For a bit of a nutty taste, try roasting the broccoli instead of steaming it.

1. Line a large pot with a half-inch of water.
2. Bring to a boil and add broccoli.
3. Cook until deep green and fork-tender, but not waterlogged and falling apart.
4. Drain broccoli and transfer to a food processor.
5. Add ½ cup of basil, garlic cloves, 1 tbsp of lemon juice, 4 tbsp of vegan Parmesan, and tofu, and blend until smooth and creamy, stopping to scrape sides as necessary.
6. Taste, adding more basil, lemon, and vegan Parmesan if desired or necessary.
7. Add salt and pepper and set aside.
8. Cook pasta according to package directions and drain.
9. Immediately add broccoli pesto, stirring to combine.
10. If you find the pasta is too dry or you prefer a more complex dimension of pesto flavor, stir in a little marinara sauce.
11. Sprinkle with additional vegan Parmesan before serving if desired.

NUTRITIONAL INFORMATION 🥢 Calories **568**; Calories from Fat **39**; Total Fat **4.4g**; Cholesterol **0mg**; Total Carbohydrate **100.3g**; Dietary Fiber **13.8g**; Sugars **7.0g**; Protein **32.4g**

Baked Ziti

Serves 4 | The quintessential comfort food of my childhood made healthy and vegan.

6 oz uncooked whole-wheat
  or brown rice ziti
2½ c tomato and basil
  marinara sauce
salt, to taste
pepper, to taste
1 recipe TVP Beef
  Crumbles (pg. 140)
1 recipe Pizza Cheese
  (pg. 242)

1. Preheat oven to 350°F.
2. Grease 8-inch casserole dish and set aside.
3. Cook pasta al dente according to package directions.
4. Drain and immediately toss with marinara.
5. Add salt and pepper, then mix in TVP.
6. Transfer to prepared casserole dish and bake for 20 minutes.
7. Pour cheese sauce (from Pizza Cheese recipe) over top and bake for another 10 minutes.

Spicy Sausage and Penne

Serves 2 to 4 | This dish is a great way to use up leftover Spicy Sausage (pg. 150) and because it comes together as fast as you can boil pasta, it's also a terrific weeknight meal.

8 oz whole-wheat penne,
  uncooked
1 c marinara sauce
2 Spicy Sausage (pg. 150),
  sliced thick
cooked spinach or chard, as
  desired (optional)
vegan Parmesan
pepper, to taste

1. Cook pasta according to package directions, then drain.
2. Immediately add marinara, stirring to ensure all pasta is evenly covered.
3. Mix in Spicy Sausage and spinach or chard, if using.
4. Generously sprinkle vegan Parmesan and pepper over top before serving.

NUTRITIONAL INFORMATION

BAKED ZITI Calories **329.8**; Calories from Fat **31.5**; Fat **3.5g**; Cholesterol **0mg**;
Total Carbohydrate **56.7g**; Dietary Fiber **11.3g**; Sugars **11.3g**; Protein **16.1g**

SPICY SAUSAGE & PENNE Calories **349**; Calories from Fat **15**; Total Fat **1.7g**;
Cholesterol **0mg**; Total Carbohydrate **57.1g**; Dietary Fiber **9.8g**; Sugars **5.4g**; Protein **28.7g**

Fettuccine Alfredo

Serves 4 | *Pictured on pg. 154* | This Alfredo comes together in an instant and is perfect when you're in the mood for a rich and creamy pasta dish. The sauce is also great over broccoli or served as an appetizer with crusty bread. I also like to add 2 cups of cooked peas to this recipe for added nutrition and overall presentation.

8 oz uncooked whole-wheat or brown rice fettuccine

1 12.3-oz package Mori-Nu tofu

1 c non-dairy milk

¼ tsp granulated garlic powder

¼ tsp granulated onion powder

¼ tsp ground nutmeg

⅛ tsp fine salt

pepper, to taste

dash of cayenne powder

¼ c nutritional yeast

1 tbsp vegan Parmesan (optional)

fresh pepper

2 tbsp chopped fresh parsley (optional)

2 tbsp Bacon Bits (pg. 137)

> **CHEF'S NOTE:**
> *Drained silken tofu may be substituted for the Mori-Nu.*

1. Cook pasta according to package directions, then drain and set aside.

2. Combine tofu, non-dairy milk, garlic and onion powders, nutmeg, salt, pepper, and cayenne powder in a food processor and blend until smooth and creamy.

3. Transfer to a saucepan and whisk in nutritional yeast and vegan Parmesan if using.

4. Heat sauce over medium heat and allow it to thicken.

5. Taste, adjusting seasonings and vegan Parmesan as needed.

6. Add pasta and peas or other vegetables, if using, and stir to coat.

7. Garnish with fresh pepper, parsley, and Bacon Bits.

VARIATION

Pasta Venice Cook one 10-oz package of frozen spinach according to directions, squeezing out any excess water. Sprinkle with 1 tbsp of garlic powder and 2 tsp of lemon juice and set aside. Drain 1 15-oz can of diced tomatoes. Toss cooked spinach, tomatoes, and ⅓ cup of Bacon Bits (pg. 137) with cooked pasta and Alfredo sauce and omit parsley.

NUTRITIONAL INFORMATION Calories **247**; Calories from Fat **19**; Total Fat **2.1g**; Cholesterol **0mg**; Total Carbohydrate **39.1g**; Dietary Fiber **7.8g**; Sugars **1.8g**; Protein **16.5g**

Spaghetti and Meatless Balls

Serves 8 | Pictured opposite | My grandmother was known for her meatballs. While her recipe was far from vegan, I know these meatless balls would make her proud. Her secret ingredients were breadcrumbs and Parmesan cheese, which I've included here. These meatless balls are also great on a sandwich, fried up as a burger, or tossed into the Tomato and Spaghetti Squash Soup (pg. 67), or in the Meatball Sub (pg. 109).

1 14-oz package Gimme
    Lean Beef Style
½ c Breadcrumbs (pg. 284)
½ c non-dairy milk
2 tbsp ketchup
2 tbsp prepared yellow
    mustard
1 tsp Italian seasoning
2 tbsp vegan Parmesan or
    nutritional yeast
½ tsp soy sauce
¼ tsp pepper
few light dashes of
    granulated garlic powder
1 tsp onion flakes (optional)
cooked spaghetti

1. Preheat the oven to 350°F.
2. Combine all ingredients by hand in a large bowl.
3. Mold mixture into a large ball with clean hands.
4. Break off walnut-sized pieces of the mixture and roll them into small balls.
5. Place on a greased or nonstick cookie sheet.
6. Bake for 10 minutes or until warm and dry on the inside. For a moister meatless ball, bake in a pan loosely covered with foil.
7. Place atop cooked spaghetti and garnish as desired.

CHEF'S NOTE: *Allow the Gimme Lean to sit out for 30 minutes to 1 hour (optional).*

NUTRITIONAL INFORMATION ➤ Calories **79**; Calories from Fat **6**; Total Fat **0.7g**; Cholesterol **0mg**; Sodium **403mg**; Total Carbohydrate **8.5g**; Dietary Fiber **2.4g**; Sugars **2.6g**; Protein **9.3g**

Enchilada Casserole

Serves 4 | A quick one-pot wonder that's perfect for potlucks and weeknight dinners.

Enchilada Sauce (pg. 260),
  divided
1 15-oz can black beans,
  drained and rinsed
2 c frozen yellow corn
1 4-oz can sliced black
  olives, divided
1 4-oz can green chilies,
  diced (optional)
12 6-inch corn tortillas,
  cut in half, divided
Quick Queso Sauce
  (pg. 263)

1. Prepare Enchilada Sauce.
2. Preheat oven to 350°F.
3. In a mixing bowl, combine beans, corn, half of the black olives, and green chilies, if using.
4. Line the bottom of a 9-inch square casserole dish with 8 tortilla slices, overlapping edges as needed.
5. Pour a portion of the enchilada sauce over tortilla slices, ensuring total distribution and that everything is covered.
6. Spoon half of the black bean mixture over top and pour enchilada sauce over to completely cover. You should have used about ⅓ of the sauce by this point.
7. Add another layer of 8 tortilla slices and cover with sauce.
8. Add the remaining bean mixture and cover with sauce.
9. Add a third top layer of tortillas and cover with the last of the sauce.
10. Sprinkle the remaining sliced olives over top and bake for 30 to 35 minutes.
11. Meanwhile, prepare Quick Queso Sauce.
12. Spoon sauce generously over plated servings of the casserole.

NUTRITIONAL INFORMATION Calories **394.5**; Calories from Fat **69.8**; Total Fat **7.7g**; Cholesterol **0mg**; Total Carbohydrate **72g**; Dietary Fiber **12.3g**; Sugars **7g**; Protein **16.5g**

Tamale Casserole

Serves 4 | Authentic tamales are far from healthy, and the corn husks can be difficult to work with. This recipe is not only healthy, it's very easy to prepare and it's still jam-packed with all the authentic Mexican flavors that make tamales so delicious. Complete this meal by serving it with Mexican Chorizo (pg. 147) and Spicy Greens (pg. 184).

1 c chopped onion
4 garlic cloves, minced
1 green bell pepper,
   seeded and diced
½ c mild salsa
½ c frozen yellow corn
½ c canned or cooked
   black beans
¼ c sliced black olives
1 tbsp chili powder
1 tsp dried oregano
1 tsp ground cumin
1 recipe Cornbread
   batter, not cooked
   (pg. 49), divided
hot sauce
salsa

1. Preheat oven to 400°F.
2. Combine onion, garlic, and bell pepper in ¼ cup of water in a saucepan over medium heat.
3. Cook until water has mostly or completely evaporated and the onions are translucent.
4. Combine all ingredients except Cornbread batter in a medium bowl and mix well to combine.
5. Spoon mixture into a greased pie or casserole dish.
6. Pat down firmly with a spatula.
7. Divide Cornbread batter in half, reserving half to make muffins or a small loaf later.
8. Pour remaining half over top of mixture in a thin layer. Don't attempt to overfill with excess batter because it won't cook evenly and the casserole will be too bready.
9. Bake for 20 to 25 minutes, until a toothpick inserted into the center comes out clean.
10. Serve with hot sauce and room-temperature salsa.

NUTRITIONAL INFORMATION Calories **259**; Calories from Fat **21.5**; Total Fat **2.4g**; Cholesterol **0mg**; Total Carbohydrate **53.4g**; Dietary Fiber **6.8g**; Sugars **5.6g**; Protein **8.6g**

Mix & Match: Vegetables, Grains, & Beans

Balsamic Braised Asparagus

Serves 4 | *Pictured opposite* | My husband's former roommate turned me on to cooking with dressing. He marinated his meats in dressings, and so I tried it with tofu. One good experiment led to another and now I'm cooking with dressings every chance I get. I love fresh asparagus when it's in season, and the tang of balsamic vinegar complements asparagus beautifully. You can also substitute a good-quality balsamic vinegar for the dressing if you prefer.

1 bunch asparagus
salt, to taste
pepper, to taste
fat-free balsamic
   vinaigrette

1. Preheat oven to 425°F.
2. Trim woody bottoms off of asparagus, about the bottom one-third.
3. Place asparagus in a 13 x 9-inch baking dish, spear heads facing each other in the center.
4. Lightly spray with cooking spray, flip, and lightly spray again.
5. Sprinkle with salt and pepper as desired and bake for 15 minutes, or until bright green and fork-tender. You may cook them longer if you prefer a more tender asparagus.
6. Once plated drizzle with balsamic vinaigrette.

NUTRITIONAL INFORMATION  Calories **28**; Calories from Fat **1**; Total Fat **0.1g**; Cholesterol **0mg**; Total Carbohydrate **6.4g**; Dietary Fiber **2.4g**; Sugars **3.1g**; Protein **2.5g**

Corn Pudding Ⓖ

Serves 4 | Don't be fooled by the term "pudding." The texture of this Appalachian dish is more like creamed corn meets quiche than that of dessert pudding. The outer layer is just firm enough that you can cut into it like a quiche, but it becomes smooth and velvety once you take a bite. It's so rich and decadent you'll deny it's healthy. Serve it with Spicy Greens (pg. 184), Charleston Red Rice (pg. 192), Southern-Style BBQ (pg. 256), or with a Salty Dog Salad (pg. 181).

3 c frozen yellow corn, thawed, divided
½ c silken tofu, drained if necessary
2 tbsp non-dairy milk
1 small sweet onion, diced
1 to 2 jalapeños, seeded and diced
1 to 1½ tsp ground ginger (optional)
cayenne powder, to taste
½ tsp turmeric
¼ c quinoa or chickpea flour
salt, to taste
pepper, to taste

1. Preheat oven to 350°F. Lightly grease a shallow 9-inch pie dish and set aside.

2. Combine ¾ cup of corn with tofu and non-dairy milk in a blender and pulse until smooth and creamy.

3. Transfer to a large mixing bowl and set aside.

4. Line a large skillet with a thin layer of water and cook onion, jalapeño, and ginger until onion becomes translucent, about 3 minutes.

5. In a mixing bowl, mix all ingredients together until well combined and pour into pie dish.

6. Use a spatula to evenly spread mixture and pack it down tightly.

7. Bake for 30 minutes or until fully cooked and bright yellow.

8. Allow to cool 10 to 15 minutes before serving.

CHEF'S NOTE: *Quinoa flour has a nutty and light taste to it that complements corn beautifully, while chickpea flour imparts a nice egg-like taste. However, any flour, including cornmeal, can be substituted if you're in a pinch.*

NUTRITIONAL INFORMATION ✎ Calories **159**; Calories from Fat **21**; Total Fat **2.3g**; Cholesterol **0mg**; Total Carbohydrate **31.1g**; Dietary Fiber **4.2g**; Sugars **4.8g**; Protein **7.6g**

Maple-Glazed Vegetables

Serves 2 | *Pictured opposite* | If you want to see an anti-vegetable family member wolf down a plate of veggies like a bowl of ice cream, make them this! I prefer to use carrots and parsnips, but it's great with butternut squash and potatoes, too.

1 tsp cornstarch
1 c vegetable broth
2 c chopped vegetables
2 tbsp pure maple syrup
1 tbsp apple cider vinegar
1 tbsp low-sodium soy
    sauce
2 tsp lemon juice
1 garlic clove, minced
pepper, to taste
1 tbsp agave nectar
    (optional)
sesame seeds (optional)

1. Mix cornstarch into 1 tsp of water, stirring until dissolved, and set aside.
2. Add broth and vegetables to a large frying pan and bring to a boil.
3. Reduce heat to low and add maple syrup, apple cider vinegar, soy sauce, juice, garlic, pepper, and agave, if using.
4. Cook for 5 minutes or until vegetables are cooked but still crisp.
5. Add cornstarch mixture and stir to combine.
6. Turn up heat and wait for the sauce to thicken, but keep a watchful eye.
7. Once the mixture is thick like a glaze, remove from heat.
8. Garnish with sesame seeds if desired.

NUTRITIONAL INFORMATION (PER SERVING) Calories **107**; Calories from Fat **4**; Total Fat **0.4g**; Cholesterol **0mg**; Total Carbohydrate **24.8g**; Dietary Fiber **2.4g**; Sugars **14.2g**; Protein **3.1g**

Baked Onion Rings

Makes 30 to 40 rings | *Pictured opposite* | I daresay I like these better than the greasy, deep-fried kind. Serve with Black Bean Burgers (pg. 86), Mushroom Burgers (pg. 89), or Tempeh Joes (pg. 111).

1 large Vidalia onion
½ c Breadcrumbs (pg. 284)
½ c yellow cornmeal
1 tsp fine salt
1 tsp granulated onion
    powder
1 tsp granulated garlic
    powder
½ c chickpea flour
½ c non-dairy milk
salt, as needed

VARIATIONS

Herbed Onion Rings
    Add 2 tsp of
Italian seasoning.

Texan Onion Rings
    Add 1 tsp of
cayenne powder, or
to taste.

1. Preheat oven 400°F.

2. Grease a large baking sheet or line with parchment paper and set aside.

3. Cut onion into ⅓-inch-thick rings, reserving all large and medium rings, about 30 to 40 rings, and store the smaller pieces for another use.

4. Grind down Breadcrumbs and cornmeal in mortar and pestle into a fine sand-like consistency.

5. Whisk Breadcrumb/cornmeal mixture, salt, and spices together in a bowl and set aside.

6. Pour chickpea flour in another bowl and non-dairy milk in a third bowl.

7. Place the bowls together in a triangle, with the non-dairy milk bowl pointing at you in the center.

8. Fully dip a ring in the non-dairy milk, twirl it in chickpea flour until coated, then quickly dip back into the non-dairy milk and immediately dredge in crumb mixture until evenly coated.

9. Place on cookie sheet and repeat with all rings.

10. Bake for 10 to 15 minutes until crisp and golden with a few light-brown spots on the edges, careful not to overcook or burn.

11. Sprinkle with salt and serve fresh out of the oven when the onions are still soft.

NUTRITIONAL INFORMATION (PER SERVING: ABOUT 5 TO 7 RINGS)
Calories **88**; Calories from Fat **10**; Total Fat **1.1g**; Total Carbohydrate **16.3g**; Dietary Fiber **1.9g**; Sugars **2.3g**; Protein **3.4g**

Rustic Yam Fries

Serves 2 | *Pictured opposite* | You could convert anyone to a low-fat vegan diet with these fries. Serve with Black Bean Burgers (pg. 86) or Soul Burgers (pg. 90).

1 medium yam or
    sweet potato
about 2 tsp Chinese 5-spice
    powder
about 1 tsp ground cumin
about ¼ tsp cayenne powder
salt, to taste
pepper, to taste

1. Preheat oven to 400°F.
2. Slice yam into very thin strips and transfer to a mixing bowl.
3. Spray with cooking spray and sprinkle spices over top with salt and pepper.
4. Mix with your hands, then re-spray and sprinkle spices a second time.
5. Mix again and repeat 2 more times with cooking spray but no seasoning.
6. Continue to toss and mix until fries are evenly coated with spices.
7. Transfer to a nonstick or greased cookie sheet and spread out in a thin layer.
8. Bake for 7 minutes.
9. Pull out, flip fries, re-spray, and bake for another 5 to 7 minutes, or until fully cooked and crisp, careful not to burn.

VARIATION

Indian-Spiced Yam Fries

Substitute garam masala for the Chinese 5-spice.

NUTRITIONAL INFORMATION Calories **60**; Calories from Fat **2**; Total Fat **0.2g**; Cholesterol **0mg**; Total Carbohydrate **13.7g**; Dietary Fiber **2.2g**; Sugars **2.7g**; Protein **1.2g**

Salty Dog Salad

Serves 4 | *Pictured opposite* | This dish is a great way to try raw kale for the first time and an excellent alternative to the usual salad. For a more colorful presentation, add cherry or grape tomatoes. I also like to eat the entire batch tossed with fresh peach slices for a light meal in the summer.

1   bunch dinosaur kale
¼ tsp fine sea salt, or
   to taste

1. Rip the leaves away from the kale stems and then discard stems. (If you have dogs, try giving them a stem; my pugs go bonkers for kale stems, hence the name!)
2. Place all the leaves in a bowl on top of each other.
3. Grab the leaves with both of your hands and twist apart, like you're wringing water out of a towel.
4. Release the leaves and pick up again, repeating the wringing motion.
5. Repeat another few times, until the leaves have been torn into bite-sized pieces.
6. Sprinkle salt over top and then toss with your hands so all of the leaves are evenly coated.
7. Add more salt if necessary or desired.
8. Let the salad rest for 5 to 10 minutes before serving (optional).

CHEF'S NOTE: *Dinosaur kale is deep green and long, compared to other kales that are not as dark and are more curly and bushy, somewhat like parsley.*

NUTRITIONAL INFORMATION 🥄 Calories **50**; Calories from Fat **6.3**; Total Fat **0.7g**; Cholesterol **0mg**; Total Carbohydrate **10g**; Dietary Fiber **2g**; Sugars **0g**; Protein **3.3g**

Southwestern Macaroni Salad

Serves 12 | *Pictured opposite* | This is not your average boring and fatty macaroni salad. It has more veggies than pasta, no fat, and a lot of heat to jazz it right up into the twenty-first century.

1¼ c uncooked brown
    rice macaroni
2 c frozen yellow corn,
    thawed
1 red bell pepper, seeded
    and diced
1 green bell pepper, seeded
    and diced
1 large tomato, diced
⅓ c Mayo (pg. 271)
½ tsp chipotle powder
salt, to taste

1. Cook pasta according to package directions and immediately rinse with cold water.

2. Mix all ingredients in a large bowl until evenly combined.

3. Chill for at least 2 hours before serving.

OPTIONAL ADDITIONS: Diced avocado, lime juice, lime zest, diced red or sweet onion, and/or a few drops of liquid smoke.

NUTRITIONAL INFORMATION Calories **65**; Calories from Fat **5**; Total Fat **0.6g**; Cholesterol **0mg**; Total Carbohydrate **13.3g**; Dietary Fiber **2.0g**; Sugars **2.6g**; Protein **2.6g**

Spicy Greens

Serves 2 | *Pictured opposite* | The first time my Southern husband brought collard greens home I cocked my head sideways and said, "What are these big green elephant ear things?" Little did I know that collard greens would soon be my favorite leafy green. Full of protein, iron, calcium, omega-3 fatty acids, and every vitamin under the sun, collard greens are the bomb. Serve them with Southern-Style BBQ (pg. 256), Charleston Red Rice (pg. 192) and Cornbread (pg. 49), or tossed with Spicy Sausage (pg. 150).

1 bunch collard greens
1 sweet onion, sliced
4 garlic cloves, thinly sliced
½ tsp red pepper flakes, or
    to taste
salt, to taste
hot sauce

1. To remove the tough stems of the collard greens, take a sharp knife and run it along the edge of each side of the stem, separating it from its leaf.

2. Then turn the knife lengthwise, cutting the collard leaves into ½-inch-wide strips.

3. Line a large skillet with ½ cup of water.

4. Add collards, onion, garlic, and red pepper flakes.

5. Cover and cook over high heat until water starts to boil.

6. Reduce heat to medium, cover, and continue to cook, incorporating and mixing ingredients with tongs every minute or so.

7. Cook until collards are dark green and onion is translucent, about 5 to 10 minutes.

8. Turn off heat, drain off any excess water, and add salt to taste.

9. Serve with hot sauce on the table for drizzling.

NUTRITIONAL INFORMATION 🍴 Calories **102**; Calories from Fat **1**; Total Fat **0.1g**; Cholesterol **0mg**; Total Carbohydrate **21.3g**; Dietary Fiber **9.6g**; Sugars **2.4g**; Protein **6.7g**

Low-Country Cucumber Salad

Serves 4 | These cucumbers are commonly served with sandwiches instead of French fries in the South. I serve them any time I'm eating Southern-Style BBQ (pg. 256) but they go well with any Southern-inspired meals and are always a big hit at potlucks.

1 large cucumber, thinly
   sliced
½ c distilled white vinegar
red pepper flakes
2 tsp hot sauce, or to taste

1. Place cucumber slices in a casserole dish.

2. Whisk ½ cup of water, vinegar, red pepper flakes, and hot sauce together and pour over cucumbers.

3. Cover and chill for at least 1 hour.

NUTRITIONAL INFORMATION 🥄 Calories **18**; Calories from Fat **1**; Total Fat **0.1g**; Cholesterol **0mg**; Total Carbohydrate **3.1g**; Sugars **1.4g**; Protein **0.5g**

Veggie Slaw

Serves 2 | This rustic coleslaw is rich, creamy, and delicious. It goes perfectly on top of salad, spread on crackers, as a side dish to summer meals, or slathered into a veggie sandwich as a condiment.

¼ c shredded carrots
½ c shredded zucchini
1 to 5 tbsp Mayo (pg. 271)
dash of granulated
   garlic powder
pinch of onion flakes
salt, to taste
pepper, to taste

1 Combine Mayo with spices, then stir in vegetables.

2 Add salt and pepper, then serve immediately.

CHEF'S NOTE: *Do not let sit; slaw will become very watery.*

NUTRITIONAL INFORMATION Calories **16**; Calories from Fat **1**; Total Fat **0.1g**; Cholesterol **0mg**; Total Carbohydrate **3.5g**; Dietary Fiber **0.7g**; Sugars **1.7g**; Protein **1.0g**

Potato Salad

Serves 6 | *Pictured opposite and on pg. 168* | Lemon and dill go together like peas and carrots. Really, it's kind of amazing.

1 lb red potatoes, cubed or
   diced
2 tbsp Dijon mustard
⅓ c Mayo (pg. 271)
¼ c chopped fresh dill
1 to 2 tsp lemon zest
crumbled vegan bacon
   (optional)
pepper, to taste
fresh dill sprigs (optional)

1. Bring a large pot of water to a boil.
2. Add potatoes and cook until fork-tender.
3. Immediately rinse potatoes with cold water and allow to completely cool.
4. Once room temperature, mix all ingredients, except pepper and optional dill sprigs, together in a large bowl.
5. Add pepper.
6. Chill before serving and garnish with fresh dill sprigs.

NUTRITIONAL INFORMATION 🥄 Calories **70**; Calories from Fat **4**; Total Fat **0.4g**; Cholesterol **0mg**; Total Carbohydrate **15.2g**; Dietary Fiber **1.7g**; Sugars **1.7g**; Protein **2.9g**

Dirty Mashed Potatoes

Serves 2 | *Pictured on pg. 134* | I call these mashed potatoes "dirty" because I leave the skins on for added texture and nutrients (and because I'm lazy). Made without butter, cream, milk, or sour cream, these mashed potatoes are still the best on the block and you can happily go back for seconds guilt-free! After you've made the basic recipe, try the variations. The Herbed Mashed Potatoes go perfectly with steamed green beans, while asparagus is the perfect contrast to the Dijon Mashed Potatoes. Serve the Cheesy Mashed Potatoes with mixed vegetables such as peas, carrots, and corn, or mixed with Bacon Bits (pg. 137).

2 Russet potatoes or 6 red
    potatoes, cubed
non-dairy milk, as needed
2 tbsp granulated garlic
    powder
1 tbsp onion flakes
salt, to taste
pepper, to taste

1. Bring a large pot of water to a boil.
2. Add potatoes and cook until fork-tender but not waterlogged, about 8 minutes.
3. Drain potatoes and return to the pot. Add a splash of non-dairy milk and spices.
4. Blend everything together using an electric mixer or potato masher.
5. Add more non-dairy milk as necessary to achieve desired consistency.
6. Add salt and pepper.

VARIATIONS

Cheesy Mashed Potatoes Add ¼ cup of nutritional yeast

Herbed Mashed Potatoes Add a few dashes of chopped fresh parsley, oregano, thyme, and/or tarragon.

Dijon Mashed Potatoes Omit garlic and onion and add 2 to 3 tbsp of Dijon mustard.

NUTRITIONAL INFORMATION Calories **192**; Calories from Fat **5**; Total Fat **0.5g**; Cholesterol **0mg**; Total Carbohydrate **42.6g**; Dietary Fiber **6.3g**; Sugars **6.2g**; Protein **6.0g**

Twice-Baked Potatoes

Serves 4 | These taste just like the high-fat kind but are completely guiltless and healthy. Serve as an appetizer or a side dish to the Mushroom Burgers (pg. 89).

2 large baking potatoes
¼ c non-dairy milk
½ tsp granulated garlic powder
½ tsp granulated onion powder
1 recipe Cheddar Cheesy Sauce (pg. 264)
1 bunch green onions, thinly sliced, green parts only
1 recipe Bacon Bits (pg. 137)
green onions, chopped (optional)

1. Preheat oven to 400°F.
2. Pierce potatoes with a fork and bake for 1 hour or until tender, when you can easily stick a fork in the potato. Cool slightly, just enough to handle without burning your hands.
3. Cut each potato in half lengthwise.
4. Scoop the inside potato out, leaving a ¼-inch-thick shell.
5. Mash potato pulp with a masher. Add non-dairy milk and spices, using a spatula to combine.
6. Spoon potato mixture back into shells and return to oven.
7. Bake for 10 to 15 minutes, or until warmed thoroughly.
8. Spoon Cheddar Cheesy Sauce over top, then sprinkle with bacon and green onion before serving.

NUTRITIONAL INFORMATION ⬛ Calories **427.5**; Calories from Fat **16**; Total Fat **1.8g**; Cholesterol **0mg**; Total Carbohydrate **84.4g**; Dietary Fiber **13.6g**; Sugars **7.5g**; Protein **20.6g**

Charleston Red Rice

Serves 4 | *Pictured opposite* | Red rice is a low-country classic. It presents beautifully, whips up instantly, and complements any dish it's served with. I've recreated the traditional recipe to be healthy and vegan, but the taste is spot-on and—dare I say it?—even better. I call it "Charleston Red Rice" as an ode to the city I called home for four years.

3 to 4 tbsp tomato paste
½ tsp granulated garlic
    powder
½ tsp granulated onion
    powder
2 c cooked brown rice
cayenne powder, to taste
hot sauce, to taste
salt, to taste
pepper, to taste

1. Mix tomato paste, garlic powder, and onion powder with warm brown rice, freshly cooked or reheated, stirring to combine.
2. Add cayenne, hot sauce, and salt and pepper.

Dirty Rice

Serves 4 | Straight from the bayou but without chicken liver or giblets. Toss with Bacon Bits (pg. 137) and serve over a plate of greens or with Cajun Meatloaf (pg. 141).

1 c uncooked brown rice
2 c vegetable broth
1 small onion, finely diced
4 garlic cloves, minced
2 celery stalks, finely diced
2 bell peppers (1 green,
    1 red), seeded and diced
1 to 2 tsp Cajun Essence
    (pg. 274)

1. Cook rice in vegetable broth for 40 to 50 minutes, or until all liquid has evaporated.
2. Ten minutes before the rice is done, cook onion in a skillet in a thin layer of water until translucent.
3. Add remaining ingredients to onion, plus water as necessary. Cook until vegetables are tender.
4. Toss vegetables with cooked rice and serve.

NUTRITIONAL INFORMATION

CHARLESTON RED RICE Calories **121**; Calories from Fat **8**; Total Fat **0.9g**; Cholesterol **0mg**; Total Carbohydrate **25.7g**; Dietary Fiber **2.3g**; Sugars **1.7g**; Protein **2.9g**

DIRTY RICE Calories **96**; Calories from Fat **6**; Total Fat **0.6g**; Cholesterol **0mg**; Total Carbohydrate **20.4g**; Dietary Fiber **2.6g**; Sugars **3.9g**; Protein **2.2g**

Traditional Stuffing Ⓢ ✪

Serves 8 | *Pictured opposite* | This dish is for the two men in my life who live and die for stuffing. Serve it alongside steamed green beans, Dirty Mashed Potatoes (pg. 190), Cornbread (pg. 49), Cranberry Sauce (pg. 267), and Torkey (Tofu Turkey) (pg. 152) at Thanksvegan, err... Thanksgiving.

6 c cubed whole-wheat bread
1⅛ tsp dried oregano
1½ tsp dried thyme
1½ tsp dried parsley
1½ tsp dried basil
1⅓ tsp powdered sage
1 large onion, chopped
4 celery stalks, chopped
1 c vegetable or No-Chicken Broth (pg. 281)

1. Leave bread cubes out overnight so they become hard and stale.

2. Preheat oven 350°F and lightly grease a 9-inch square baking pan; set aside.

3. Transfer bread cubes to a plastic bag, spray once or twice with cooking spray, add herbs, and toss for a minute.

4. Open bag and re-spray once or twice, then seal it and shake again until cubes are evenly coated and set aside.

5. Cook celery and onion in ½ cup of water over medium heat until celery is soft, onion is translucent and most of the water has evaporated, about 5 minutes.

6. Transfer to a large bowl and combine with bread cubes.

7. Stir to combine, then transfer to prepared pan.

8. Drizzle with ¼ cup of broth or less.

9. Bake for 30 minutes, checking every 10 minutes, and adding more No-Chicken Broth as necessary, to prevent stuffing from drying out.

OPTIONAL ADDITIONS: 1 cup of chopped apple, 1 cup of dried cranberries soaked overnight in fresh orange juice, 1 cup of chopped chestnuts or walnuts, 1 cup of sliced mushrooms, or 12 ounces of cooked vegan sausage, crumbled

NUTRITIONAL INFORMATION 🥄 Calories **115**; Calories from Fat **13**; Total Fat **1.4g**; Cholesterol **0mg**; Total Carbohydrate **20.0g**; Dietary Fiber **3.3g**; Sugars **3.4g**; Protein **5.7g**

Cornbread Stuffing with Chorizo

Serves 4 | Last Thanksgiving I wanted to be a little edgy, so I reinvented the quintessential side dish by giving it a Mexican-inspired makeover. Let's just say that stuffing has never felt so sassy!

2 c cubed Cornbread
   (pg. 49)
2 c cubed whole-wheat
   bread
2 celery stalks, sliced
1 sweet onion, diced
2 c Mexican Chorizo
   (pg. 147)
½ c vegetable broth

1. Leave both types of bread out overnight so the cubes become hard and stale.

2. Preheat oven to 350°F and lightly grease a 9-inch square baking pan; set aside.

3. Cook celery and onion in ¼ cup of water until celery is soft and onion is translucent, about 4 minutes.

4. Add Mexican Chorizo, stirring to combine.

5. Transfer chorizo mixture to a large bowl and mix with bread and cornbread.

6. Transfer to pan and bake for 30 minutes, checking every 10 minutes and drizzling with vegetable broth as needed to keep stuffing slightly moist, but not soggy.

> **CHEF'S NOTE:** *Although not fat-free, you can use 12 ounces of store-bought vegan chorizo to save time.*

NUTRITIONAL INFORMATION 🍴 Calories **444.8**; Calories from Fat **40.5**; Fat **4.5g**; Cholesterol **0mg**; Total Carbohydrate **80.7g**; Dietary Fiber **14g**; Sugars **7.5g**; Protein **24.1g**

Dijon-Herb Green Beans

Serves 2 | I love green beans, and this recipe is my favorite way to eat them. It's healthy, flavorful, and goes perfectly with a big ol' plate of Dirty Mashed Potatoes (pg. 190) and chickpeas. I lovingly refer to that dish as "Chickpea à la Queen," and it's one of our regular weeknight meals. By the way, any green herb will do in this recipe, but some of my favorites are thyme, basil, tarragon, parsley, dill, oregano, or rosemary.

½ lb green beans, trimmed
1 heaping tsp cornstarch
1 c vegetable broth
1 tbsp Dijon mustard
1 to 2 tsp lemon juice
1¼ tsp onion flakes
⅛ tsp granulated garlic
    powder
a dash or pinch of every
    dried green herb
    you've got
salt, to taste
pepper, to taste

1. Steam green beans until cooked but still slightly crisp and deep green in color.

2. Once the green beans are cooked, whisk cornstarch with broth and Dijon mustard.

3. Pour Dijon mixture into a skillet and add remaining ingredients, except green beans, salt, and pepper.

4. Bring to a boil, then reduce heat to low and allow it to thicken into a glaze.

5. Add salt and pepper, toss with green beans, and serve.

> **CHEF'S NOTE:** *To assemble "Chickpea à la Queen"*
> *Make a big bed of mashed potatoes in the middle of the*
> *plate. Place green beans over the potatoes, then add*
> *chickpeas on top and around the potatoes.*

NUTRITIONAL INFORMATION ✎ Calories **60**; Calories from Fat **4**; Total Fat **0.4g**; Cholesterol **0mg**; Total Carbohydrate **13.4g**; Dietary Fiber **4.2g**; Sugars **2.6g**; Protein **2.5g**

Baked Beans

Serves 4 | *Pictured opposite* | I'd never had homemade baked beans until I was in England, where they were served to me at breakfast, over toast. Even though 7 a.m. isn't exactly the time of day I usually like to eat baked beans, I couldn't get over how much better they were than the canned variety I grew up with. Serve with Mushroom Burgers (pg. 89) or tofu dogs, Cornbread (pg. 49) and Spicy Greens (pg. 184), or at breakfast, English-style.

½ small onion, diced
1 garlic clove, minced
1 15-oz can navy beans, unrinsed
2 tbsp ketchup
2 tbsp molasses
1 tsp Dijon mustard
1 tbsp soy sauce
2 to 3 tbsp pure maple syrup
light dash of cayenne powder
salt, to taste
pepper, to taste

1. Preheat oven to 300°F.
2. Cook onion and garlic in ¼ cup of water over high heat until the onion is translucent, about 2 minutes.
3. Add remaining ingredients and bring to a boil.
4. Once boiling, remove from heat and transfer mixture to a casserole dish, cover with foil, and bake for 30 minutes.
5. Let rest for 15 minutes, allowing the sauce to thicken.
6. Stir to incorporate before serving.

> **CHEF'S NOTE:** *If your beans come out soupy, you can transfer them to a saucepan and cook them uncovered over high heat for a few minutes to reduce the liquid.*

NUTRITIONAL INFORMATION 🥄 Calories **160**; Calories from Fat **1**; Total Fat **0.1g**; Cholesterol **0mg**; Total Carbohydrate **33.9g**; Dietary Fiber **6.0g**; Sugars **13.7g**; Protein **6.3g**

Desserts

Chocolate Chip Cookies

Makes 16 cookies | *Pictured opposite* | These are the best low-fat chocolate chip cookies you'll ever eat! They're ridiculously addictive fresh out of the oven. You've been warned.

⅓ c unsweetened
  applesauce
½ c light brown sugar
1 tsp vanilla extract
¼ c non-dairy milk
1 c whole-wheat pastry
  flour
1 tsp baking powder
¼ tsp fine salt
1 tbsp cornstarch
a few dashes of ground
  cinnamon
½ c vegan chocolate chips

1. Preheat oven to 350°F.
2. Grease cookie sheet or line with parchment paper.
3. In a large bowl, combine applesauce, sugar, vanilla, and non-dairy milk.
4. In a small bowl, whisk flour, baking powder, salt, cornstarch, and cinnamon.
5. Transfer the dry mixture into the wet mixture in three batches. Stir until almost combined.
6. Fold in chips.
7. Drop spoonfuls on cookie sheet and bake for 7 to 10 minutes for a soft and light cookie or a few minutes more for a firmer cookie, being careful not to burn.

VARIATION
Double Chocolate Chip Cookies 🌸 🅢 😊 ✎ Replace 2 tbsp of flour with 2 tbsp of unsweetened cocoa.

NUTRITIONAL INFORMATION ✎ Calories **61**; Calories from Fat **6**; Total Fat **0.7g**; Cholesterol **0mg**; Total Carbohydrate **12.5g**; Dietary Fiber **1.0g**; Sugars **6.2g**; Protein **1.0g**

VARIATIONS

Chai Oatmeal Cookies 🟤 🄕 Ⓢ 〜 Add 1 tsp of ground cinnamon, ½ tsp of ground ginger, ½ tsp of ground cloves, and ¾ tsp of ground cardamom.

Nutty Oatmeal Cookies 🟤 Ⓢ 😀 〜 Add 2 tbsp of creamy smooth peanut butter, reduce applesauce to ¼ cup, omit cinnamon, and add ¼ cup of chopped peanuts.

Pumpkin-Raisin Oatmeal Cookies 🟤 🄕 Ⓢ 😀 ✪ 〜 Substitute 6 tbsp of pure canned pumpkin for applesauce, add 1 tbsp of pumpkin pie spice, and omit vanilla and cinnamon. **CHEF'S NOTE**: *Use leftover canned pumpkin to make Maple Muffins (pg. 46) or Gingerbread Mini-Loaves (pg. 51).*

Oatmeal Cookies

Makes 14 cookies | *Pictured opposite* | Chewy and yet still soft right out of the oven, these oatmeal cookies are my all-time favorite.

6 tbsp unsweetened applesauce
½ c raw sugar
¼ c pure maple syrup
½ slightly ripe banana, mashed
2 tbsp non-dairy milk
½ tsp vanilla extract
1½ c rolled oats
½ c whole-wheat flour
¼ tsp baking soda
a few dashes of ground cinnamon
¼ c raisins, cranberries, or chocolate chips (optional)

CHEF'S NOTE:
Add 1 tsp or more of ground flax seeds for a chewier cookie.

1. Preheat oven to 350°F.
2. Grease cookie sheet or line with parchment paper.
3. Mix applesauce, sugar, maple syrup, banana, non-dairy milk, and vanilla in a medium bowl.
4. In a large bowl, mix oats, flour, baking soda, and cinnamon.
5. Pour wet mixture into dry mixture, add optional raisins, cranberries, or chips, and gently stir until just combined. If not using raisins, cranberries, or chips, add 1 to 2 extra tbsp of flour.
6. Pick off bouncy ball–sized pieces and place on sheet. Alternatively, drop spoonfuls of batter onto the cookie sheet if the batter is too sticky or loose to mold into balls.
7. Flatten with palm and leave at least a ½ inch between each cookie.
8. Bake for 10 to 15 minutes, until springy to the touch or desired firmness is reached.

NUTRITIONAL INFORMATION

OATMEAL COOKIES ✦ Calories **93**; Calories from Fat **6**; Total Fat **0.7g**; Cholesterol **0mg**; Total Carbohydrate **20.5g**; Dietary Fiber **1.4g**; Sugars **11.8g**; Protein **1.6g**

PUMPKIN-RAISIN OATMEAL COOKIES ✦ Calories **92**; Calories from Fat **6**; Total Fat **0.7g**; Cholesterol **0mg**; Total Carbohydrate **20.3g**; Dietary Fiber **1.5g**; Sugars **11.4g**; Protein **1.7g**

NUTTY OATMEAL COOKIE ✦ Calories **127**; Calories from Fat **28**; Total Fat **3.0g**; Cholesterol **0mg**; Total Carbohydrate **22.7g**; Dietary Fiber **1.5g**; Sugars **11.9g**; Protein **3.0g**

Instant Cookie Dough

Serves 2 | I did a detox some years back, and one of the dessert recipes used honey, soaked oats, raw nut butter, and carob to make a "cookie dough." I've since reworked the recipe to fit my taste preferences and pantry staples. I should also mention that when I posted this recipe up for my cookbook testers, 15 of them made it within 10 minutes of posting. Smooth peanut butter can also be substituted for the Nutty Spread if you prefer.

1 c rolled oats
2 tbsp Nutty Spread
   (pg. 253)
3 tbsp pure maple syrup
2 tbsp unsweetened cocoa

1. Mix all ingredients together until well combined.
2. Eat with a spoon.

VARIATION

No-Bake Choco-Oat Cookies ⬤ Ⓕ Ⓢ ☺ ✎ Form the Instant Cookie Dough into small cookie shapes using your hands. Let cookies sit out for about an hour or until they firm up, are no longer sticky, and have the consistency of a baked cookie.

NUTRITIONAL INFORMATION ✎ Calories **285.5**; Calories from Fat **52.5**; Fat **5.9g**; Cholesterol **0mg**; Protein **8g**; Carbohydrate **55.4g**; Fiber **7g**; Sugar **3.3g**

Fudgy Brownies

Makes 9 squares | These brownies are so moist and rich that no one will believe you when you tell them they're whole-wheat, vegan, and made with no added fat!

2 c whole-wheat pastry flour
1 c brown sugar
1 c raw sugar
¾ c unsweetened cocoa
1 tsp baking powder
1 tsp fine salt
1 c water
¼ c chocolate non-dairy milk
1 8-oz cup plain soy yogurt
1 tsp vanilla extract
½ c vegan chocolate chips
  (optional)

1. Preheat oven to 350°F.

2. Grease a standard 9-inch square baking pan and set aside.

3. Whisk flour, sugars, cocoa, baking powder, and salt together in a large bowl.

4. Add 1 cup of water, chocolate non-dairy milk, soy yogurt, and vanilla, stirring until just combined.

5. Add chips if using and continue to stir until fully incorporated.

6. Transfer to the greased pan, using a spatula to even out the batter and smooth the top.

7. Bake for 30 to 40 minutes.

CHEF'S NOTE: *Fruit-flavored vegan yogurts such as strawberry and raspberry add a nice touch to these brownies. Other vegan yogurts such as rice yogurt or coconut yogurt may be used in place of soy yogurt for a soy-free brownie.*

NUTRITIONAL INFORMATION Calories **284**; Calories from Fat **15**; Total Fat **1.7g**; Saturated Fat **0.6g**; Cholesterol **0mg**; Total Carbohydrate **65.5g**; Dietary Fiber **5.2g**; Sugars **40.8g**; Protein **4.7g**

Black Bean Brownies

Makes 9 squares | *Pictured opposite* | I made these brownies for my friend Tara who heard about a non-vegan version in a Weight Watchers meeting. I posted the recipe on my website, Happyherbivore.com, half expecting everyone to shudder in horror. To my complete surprise, these brownies took food blogs and Twitter by storm. This is by far my most popular recipe.

1 15-oz can black beans, drained and rinsed
2 spotted bananas
⅓ c agave nectar
¼ c unsweetened cocoa
1 tbsp ground cinnamon
1 tsp vanilla extract
¼ cup raw sugar (optional)
¼ tsp salt (optional)
¼ cup instant oats

1. Preheat oven to 350°F.
2. Grease a standard 9-inch square pan and set aside.
3. Combine all ingredients except oats in a food processor or blender and blend until smooth, stopping and scraping the sides as needed.
4. Stir in oats and bake for approximately 30 minutes or until a toothpick inserted into the center comes out clean. Allow to cool completely before slicing.

VARIATIONS

Dark Chocolate Brownies
— Add another ¼ cup of unsweetened cocoa.

Mint Chocolate Chip Brownies
— Omit cinnamon and add a few drops of mint extract.

Mexican Hot Chocolate Brownies
— Add ¼ to ½ tsp of cayenne pepper.

Mocha Fudge Brownies
— Add 2 to 3 tsp of instant coffee granules.

CHEF'S NOTE:
The riper the banana, the sweeter it tastes and the more banana smell and flavor it has. Add the optional sugar with less ripe bananas and omit with very ripe bananas. You can also substitute chickpeas, black-eyed peas, and adzuki beans.

NUTRITIONAL INFORMATION — Calories **112**; Calories from Fat **8**; Total Fat **0.9g**; Cholesterol **0mg**; Total Carbohydrate **24.7g**; Dietary Fiber **4.8g**; Sugars **12.2g**; Protein **3.5g**

Single-Serving Brownie

Serves 1 | Oh, yes. Yes, I did.

2 tbsp whole-wheat pastry
   flour
1 tbsp vegan chocolate chips
1 tbsp light brown sugar
1 tbsp unsweetened cocoa
light dash of ground
   cinnamon
small pinch of baking
   powder
1 tbsp agave nectar
1 generous tbsp
   unsweetened applesauce
1 tsp unsweetened
   non-dairy milk
drop or 2 vanilla extract

1. Preheat oven to 350°F.
2. Grease a single muffin cup and set aside.
3. Mix flour, chocolate chips, sugar, cocoa, cinnamon, and baking powder together.
4. Stir in agave, applesauce, non-dairy milk, and vanilla until combined.
5. Bake for 15 to 20 minutes, until a toothpick inserted in the center comes out clean.

> **CHEF'S NOTE:** *Instead of using an entire muffin pan, you can put a paper liner into a 1 cup metal measuring cup. Be sure to spray the liner with your cooking spray to prevent sticking and be careful not to touch the hot measuring cup with your bare hands.*

NUTRITIONAL INFORMATION 🥄 Calories **191**; Calories from Fat **18**; Total Fat **2.0g**; Saturated Fat **0.9g**; Cholesterol **0mg**; Total Carbohydrate **43.7g**; Dietary Fiber **4.9g**; Sugars **27.7g**; Protein **3.0g**

Carrie's Vanilla Chai Cupcakes

Makes 8 cupcakes | My friend Carrie is the best tester a cook can ask for. As soon as I post a recipe, she's making it and telling me what her husband and daughters think. I knew I had to create something just for her, and this is it! I combined Carrie's love of chai lattes with vegan cupcakes. Thanks for everything, Carrie!

1 c vanilla non-dairy milk
3 chai teabags
¼ c applesauce
½ c raw sugar
1 tsp vanilla extract
1½ c whole-wheat pastry
    flour
1¼ tsp baking powder
½ tsp fine salt
1 tsp ground cinnamon
½ tsp ground ginger
½ tsp ground cloves
¼ tsp ground cardamom
Ricemellow or Cream
    Cheese Icing (pg. 223)

1. Gently warm non-dairy milk on the stove, careful not to scald it. Once it's at a near boil, turn off heat, add teabags, and steep for 4 to 6 minutes.

2. Preheat oven to 350°F. Grease a muffin tin or spray paper liners with cooking spray, then set aside.

3. Once milk is cool, remove tea bags and mix with applesauce, sugar, and vanilla in a medium bowl.

4. In a large bowl, whisk flour, baking powder, salt, and spices together.

5. Pour wet mixture into dry mixture in 3 to 4 batches, stirring until just combined.

6. Fill muffin cups ¾ full and bake for 15 to 25 minutes.

7. Remove cupcakes from oven and transfer to a wire cooling rack. Once completely cool, add icing and sprinkle with fresh nutmeg or cinnamon.

CHEF'S NOTE: *Add 1 tsp of ground cinnamon, ½ tsp of ground ginger, ½ tsp of ground cloves, and ¼ tsp of ground cardamom into the cream cheese frosting for a chai-flavored icing, or simply dust the vanilla icing with these spices before serving. Also, if you don't have vanilla non-dairy milk on hand, whisk a few drops of vanilla extract into plain non-dairy milk before you begin.*

NUTRITIONAL INFORMATION (WITHOUT ICING) ⬤ Calories **97**; Calories from Fat **4**; Total Fat **0.4g**; Cholesterol **0mg**; Total Carbohydrate **20.8g**; Dietary Fiber **1.7g**; Sugars **9.4g**; Protein **2.0g**

Carrot Cake Cupcakes Ⓕ 😀 ✪

Makes 12 cupcakes | *Pictured opposite* | Some people dream in chocolate. Me? I dream in carrot cake. I can't think of a single dessert I love more. I made these cupcakes for my first veganniversary, and they still remain one of the most popular recipes on my website, Happyherbivore.com.

1½ c whole-wheat pastry flour
1 cup raw sugar
1 tsp baking powder
1 tsp baking soda
1½ tsp ground cinnamon
½ tsp fine salt
1½ c unsweetened applesauce
1 generous tsp vanilla extract
1 large carrot, peeled and shredded
Cream Cheese Icing (pg. 223)

1. Preheat oven to 350°F.

2. Grease a muffin pan or spray paper liners.

3. In a medium bowl, whisk flour, sugar, baking powder, baking soda, cinnamon, and salt together.

4. In a large bowl, combine applesauce, vanilla, and carrot.

5. Add dry mixture to wet mixture in 3 to 4 batches, stirring until just combined.

6. Fill muffin cups ¾ full and bake for 18 to 25 minutes, or until a toothpick inserted into the center comes out clean.

7. Remove cupcakes from oven and transfer to a wire cooling rack.

8. Once completely cool, add icing and garnish with chopped walnuts or shredded carrot.

NUTRITIONAL INFORMATION (WITHOUT ICING) 🍪 Calories **137**;
Calories from Fat **3**; Total Fat **0.3g**; Cholesterol **0mg**; Total Carbohydrate **32.1g**; Dietary Fiber **2.2g**;
Sugars **20.1g**; Protein **1.6g**

Root Beer Float Cupcakes

Makes 12 cupcakes | The only thing better than a root beer float is a root beer float cupcake!

¼ c unsweetened
   applesauce
¼ c raw sugar
1 c root beer
1 tsp vanilla extract
1½ c whole-wheat pastry
   flour
1¼ tsp baking powder
½ tsp fine salt
1 pinch of ground anise
   seed (optional)
Ricemellow or Vanilla
   Icing (pg. 225)

CHEF'S NOTE:
*Soda should still
be carbonated and
not flat.*

1. Preheat oven to 350°F.

2. Grease muffin tin or spray paper cups with cooking spray and set aside.

3. In a medium bowl, whisk applesauce, sugar, root beer, and vanilla together.

4. In a large bowl, whisk flour, baking powder, salt and anise, if using, until well combined.

5. Pour the wet mixture into the dry mixture in 3 to 4 batches, stirring until just combined and using as few strokes as possible

6. Spoon batter into muffin cups ¾ full and bake for 15 to 25 minutes, or until a toothpick inserted into the center comes out clean.

7. Remove cupcakes from oven and transfer to a wire cooling rack.

8. Once completely cool, add Ricemellow or Vanilla Icing and sprinkle with fresh nutmeg or cinnamon.

NUTRITIONAL INFORMATION

ROOT BEER FLOAT CUPCAKES (WITHOUT ICING) Calories **83**;
Calories from Fat **2**; Total Fat **0.2g**; Cholesterol **0mg**; Total Carbohydrate **18.2g**; Dietary Fiber **1.6g**;
Sugars **6.9g**; Protein **1.5g**

ROOT BEER DIET FLOAT CUPCAKES—SERVES 12 (PER SERVING: 1 CUPCAKE)
(WITHOUT ICING) Calories **75**; Calories from Fat **2**; Total Fat **0.2g**; Cholesterol **0mg**;
Total Carbohydrates **16.0g**; Dietary Fiber **1.6g**; Sugars **4.7g**; Protein **1.5g**

Chocolate Cupcakes

Makes 12 cupcakes | Choco-yum-yum!

¼ c unsweetened
   applesauce
½ c raw sugar
1 c chocolate non-dairy
   milk
1 tsp vanilla extract
1¼ c whole-wheat pastry
   flour
¼ c unsweetened cocoa
1¼ tsp baking powder
⅓ tsp fine salt
½ c vegan chocolate chips
Vanilla or Peppermint
   Icing (pg. 225)
peppermints, mini candy
   canes, green or red
   sprinkles, or chocolate
   bits (optional)

1. Preheat oven to 350°F.
2. Lightly grease a muffin pan or spray paper cups with cooking spray.
3. In a large bowl, combine applesauce, sugar, non-dairy milk, and vanilla.
4. In a medium bowl, whisk flour, cocoa, baking powder, and salt.
5. Add dry mixture to wet mixture in 3 to 4 batches until almost combined.
6. Add chocolate chips and stir until just combined.
7. Spoon batter into muffin cups ¾ full and bake for 15 to 25 minutes, or until a toothpick inserted into the center comes out clean.
8. Remove cupcakes from oven and transfer to a wire cooling rack.
9. Once completely cool, add icing and garnish with peppermints, mini candy canes, green or red sprinkles, or chocolate bits.

VARIATION

Chocolate-Peppermint Cupcakes Use mint extract instead of vanilla extract and stir in 2 tbsp of crushed candy cane pieces into the batter in step 6.

NUTRITIONAL INFORMATION (WITHOUT ICING) Calories **106**; Calories from Fat **11**; Total Fat **1.3g**; Saturated Fat **0.5g**; Cholesterol **0mg**; Total Carbohydrate **22.0g**; Dietary Fiber **2.2g**; Sugars **11.3g**; Protein **2.4g**

Strawberry Cupcakes

Serves 12 | *Pictured opposite and on pg. 200* | Every year that we lived in Florida, my parents took me to the Strawberry Festival, where I ate strawberry shortcake until I started to turn pink (so that's a bit of an exaggeration, but I did eat a lot!). This is my cupcake version.

2 c whole-wheat pastry
    flour
1 tsp baking powder
½ tsp baking soda
½ tsp fine salt
¼ cup applesauce
1 c raw sugar
1 c non-dairy milk
1 tsp lemon extract or zest
1 recipe Vanilla Icing
    (pg. 225)
12 oz fresh or frozen
    strawberries

1. Preheat oven to 350°F.
2. Grease a muffin tin or spray paper liners and set aside.
3. In a medium bowl, whisk flour, baking powder, baking soda, and salt together.
4. In a large bowl, whisk applesauce, sugar, non-dairy milk, and lemon extract or zest until well combined.
5. Pour dry mixture into the wet mixture in 3 to 4 batches, stirring until just combined.
6. Spoon batter into muffin cups ¾ full and bake for 15 to 25 minutes, or until a toothpick inserted in the center comes out clean.
7. Transfer to a wire cooling rack.
8. Once the cupcakes have fully cooled, slather icing over top and garnish with fresh strawberry slices (thawed, if using frozen).

NUTRITIONAL INFORMATION (WITHOUT ICING) Calories **157.8**;
Calories from Fat **4.5**; Total Fat **0.5g**; Cholesterol **0mg**; Total Carbohydrate **35.6g**; Dietary Fiber **2.8g**; Sugars **2.8g**; Protein **2.8g**

Pumpkin Pie

Serves 9 | This pie is incredible. It's totally crustless but still firms up like the real deal so you can cut individual slices without it falling apart. It's like a little tofu miracle.

½ c silken tofu
1½ c non-dairy milk
2 tbsp cornstarch
1 tsp vanilla extract
2 c canned pure pumpkin
½ c whole-wheat pastry flour
2 tsp baking powder
½ c brown sugar
¼ tsp fine salt
3 tsp pumpkin pie spice

CHEF'S NOTE:
Mori-Nu extra-firm silken tofu works best in this recipe.

1. Preheat oven to 350°F.
2. Grease a shallow 9-inch glass pie dish and set aside.
3. In a blender or food processor, blend tofu, non-dairy milk, cornstarch, and vanilla until smooth, stopping to scrape sides periodically.
4. Add remaining ingredients and blend for about a minute more, until the mixture is uniform and well combined.
5. Pour the mixture into the pie dish and bake for 1 hour.
6. Allow the pie to cool on the counter, away from the hot oven, until room temperature.
7. Cover with plastic wrap and refrigerate overnight, or for at least 4 hours.

VARIATION

Sweet Potato Pie Substitute 2 cups of sweet potato puree for pumpkin and replace pumpkin pie spice with 1 tsp of ground cinnamon, ½ tsp of ground nutmeg, ¼ tsp of ground ginger, and a small pinch of ground cloves.

NUTRITIONAL INFORMATION

PUMPKIN PIE Calories **77**; Calories from Fat **6**; Total Fat **0.6g**; Cholesterol **0mg**; Total Carbohydrate **16.4g**; Dietary Fiber **1.9g**; Sugars **10.8g**; Protein **2.5g**

SWEET POTATO PIE Calories **84**; Calories from Fat **5**; Total Fat **0.5g**; Cholesterol **0mg**; Total Carbohydrate **17.9g**; Dietary Fiber **1.2g**; Sugars **10.2g**; Protein **2.4g**

Cheesecake ✪

Serves 9 | What kind of New Yorker would I be without my cheesecake? Yeah, I've been to Junior's. I still like this one better.

1 12.3-oz package
   Mori-Nu tofu
1 8-oz container vegan
   cream cheese
⅔ c raw sugar
¾ tsp almond extract
2 tbsp cornstarch
Graham Cracker Crust
   (pg. 222)
Blueberry Sauce
   (pg. 227; optional)

1. Preheat oven to 350°F.

2. Drain tofu and transfer to a blender along with cream cheese.

3. Blend for 30 seconds, scrape the sides, and blend for 30 seconds more.

4. Add remaining ingredients except crust and blueberry topping and blend for 3 minutes, scraping the sides periodically.

5. Pour batter into prepared crust and use a spatula to evenly distribute and smooth out the top.

6. Bake for 40 to 45 minutes, and then place on the counter away from the hot oven to cool to room temperature.

7. Chill overnight in the fridge, or for at least 10 hours.

8. Serve topped with blueberry sauce, if using.

CHEF'S NOTE: *If you don't have a strong blender or processor, leave the vegan cream cheese out for 20 to 30 minutes to soften it up. Also, any Mori-Nu tofu will do here but extra-firm is best; buy the low-fat or lite option if you can.*

NUTRITIONAL INFORMATION (WITHOUT CRUST) Calories **149**; Calories from Fat **42**; Total Fat **4.7g**; Saturated Fat **1.8g**; Cholesterol **0mg**; Total Carbohydrate **23.4g**; Sugars **16.8g**; Protein **3.6g**

Pumpkin Cheesecake

Serves 9 | *Pictured opposite* | Rich and decadent like a cheesecake but flavored like a pumpkin pie, this dessert is the perfect end to any holiday meal.

1 15-oz can pure pumpkin
   puree
1 8-oz tub vegan cream
   cheese
⅔ c light brown sugar
1 to 2 tbsp pumpkin pie spice
1 tsp vanilla extract
2 tbsp cornstarch
Graham Cracker Crust
   (pg. 222)
6 oz plain soy yogurt or
   vegan whipped cream
   (optional)
ground nutmeg or
   cinnamon for dusting

CHEF'S NOTE:
*If you don't have a
strong blender or
processor, leave the
vegan cream cheese
out for 20 to 30
minutes to soften
it up.*

1. Preheat oven to 350°F.

2. Combine pumpkin and vegan cream cheese in a blender or food processor.

3. Blend until smooth and creamy, stopping to scrape the sides as necessary.

4. Add sugar, pumpkin pie spice, vanilla, and cornstarch and blend again for three minutes, periodically stopping to scrape the sides as necessary.

5. Pour batter into prepared crust and use a spatula to evenly distribute and smooth out the top.

6. Smooth the top with a spatula and bake for 40 to 45 minutes, until fully cooked. The pie will rise during baking and should be about ½ inch higher than it started.

7. Remove from oven and place on counter, away from heat.

8. Allow pie to cool to room temperature, about 2 to 3 hours. The pie will fall as it cools; do not be alarmed.

9. Cover and chill overnight, or for at least 10 hours.

10. Before serving, slice into 9 pieces and add a dollop of soy yogurt or whipped cream to each if desired.

11. Sprinkle with nutmeg or cinnamon for garnish.

NUTRITIONAL INFORMATION (WITHOUT CRUST) Calories **156**;
Calories from Fat **42**; Total Fat **4.6g**; Saturated Fat **1.8g**; Cholesterol **0mg**; Total Carbohydrate **27.3g**;
Dietary Fiber **1.6g**; Sugars **16.2g**; Protein **1.8g**

Graham Cracker Crust

Makes 1 pie | Sadly, the graham cracker crusts at the store are usually loaded with fat and aren't whole-wheat. I've tried making my own crust at home a few ways, and this is my favorite method. It firms up and stays hard without getting soggy even as it lingers in the fridge for days.

1⅔ c whole-wheat graham
   crackers, crumbled
½ tsp ground cinnamon
7 to 8 tbsp unsweetened
   applesauce

1. Preheat oven to 350°F. Grease 9-inch pie dish and set aside.

2. Place graham crackers into a food processor and pulse until crumbles reach the consistency of coarse sand or sea salt.

3. Transfer graham cracker crumbles to a mixing bowl and whisk in cinnamon.

4. Add applesauce and stir until evenly wet and large clunks form.

5. Using your fingers, press mixture into prepared pie dish to form a crust.

6. Pack the crust down tightly and bake for 8 minutes.

7. Allow crust to completely cool before using.

> **CHEF'S NOTE:** *Substitute any flavored graham crackers you like: chocolate, vanilla, or ginger.*

NUTRITIONAL INFORMATION 🍴 Calories **107**; Calories from Fat **23**; Total Fat **2.5g**; Cholesterol **0mg**; Total Carbohydrate **19.9g**; Dietary Fiber **2.7g**; Sugars **3.7g**; Protein **2.6g**

Cream Cheese Icing

Serves 12

¼ c vegan cream cheese
¼ c confectioners' sugar
non-dairy milk, as needed

1. Using electric beaters, whip cream cheese with sugar until you reach a glaze consistency.

2. Add more sugar for a thicker paste, or if a sweeter icing is desired.

3. If the mixture becomes too thick, thin out with non-dairy milk.

VARIATION

Lime Cream Cheese Icing Add the juice and zest of one small lime.

Maple Icing

Serves 12 | This is so good you'll want to eat it with a spoon. Spread it on Pumpkin Bread (pg. 52) or Carrot Cake Cupcakes (pg. 213).

1 c confectioners' sugar
2 tbsp pure maple syrup
1 tsp ground cinnamon
1 tsp vanilla extract

1. Combine all ingredients together in a small bowl, whipping to combine.

2. Add more maple syrup for a thinner icing or more sugar for a thicker icing.

NUTRITIONAL INFORMATION

CREAM CHEESE ICING (PER 2 TBSP) Calories **24**; Calories from Fat **8**; Total Fat **0.8g**; Cholesterol **0mg**; Total Carbohydrate **4.0g**; Sugars **2.8g**; Protein **0.2g**

MAPLE ICING (PER 2 TBSP) Calories **49**; Calories from Fat **0**; Total Fat **0.0g**; Cholesterol **0mg**; Total Carbohydrate **12.4g**; Sugars **11.8g**; Protein **0.0g**

Vanilla Icing

Serves 12 | *Pictured opposite* | What's more classic than vanilla? You can omit the vanilla extract if you use vanilla non-dairy milk.

1 c confectioners' sugar
1 tbsp non-dairy milk
1 tsp vanilla extract
food coloring (optional)

1. Stir ingredients together to combine.
2. Add more sugar to thicken the icing or more non-dairy milk to thin it out. Ideally, you want the consistency to be a paste-like glaze.
3. Add food coloring, if desired, and slather icing onto cupcakes. Add garnishes while the icing is still wet to ensure they stick.

VARIATION
Peppermint Icing ⊘ ⊕ ⊕ ⊕ ⌢ Substitute peppermint extract for vanilla extract.

Tofu Chocolate Icing

Makes 2 cups | So chocolatey but so sinless.

1 lb silken tofu, drained
12 tbsp confectioners' sugar, divided
3 to 4 tbsp unsweetened cocoa
1 tsp vanilla extract

1. Blend tofu in a food processor or blender until smooth and creamy.
2. Add vanilla, 4 tbsp confectioners' sugar, and 2 tbsp of cocoa, then blend. Add 4 more tbsp of sugar and blend again.
3. Add 4 more tbsp of sugar and blend for a third time.
4. Taste, adding more sugar or cocoa as needed.

NUTRITIONAL INFORMATION

VANILLA ICING (PER 2 TBSP) ⌢ Calories 40; Calories from Fat 0; Total Fat **0.0g**; Cholesterol **0mg**; Total Carbohydrate **10.0g**; Sugars **9.8g**; Protein **0.0g**

TOFU CHOCOLATE ICING (PER 2 TBSP) ⌢ Calories **35**; Calories from Fat **3**; Total Fat **0.3g**; Cholesterol **0mg**; Total Carbohydrate **6.7g**; Sugars **5.7g**; Protein **1.7g**

Blueberry Sauce

Makes ½ cup, serves 4 | *Pictured opposite* | Perfect on top of Cheesecake (pg. 219), Pancakes (pg. 28), or vegan vanilla ice cream!

1 c frozen wild blueberries
agave nectar, to taste
pinch of lemon zest
2 tsp fresh lemon juice
1 tbsp cornstarch mixed
   into 1 tbsp water

1. Add berries, ½ cup of water, and agave to a saucepan and bring to a boil.
2. Add zest, lemon juice, and cornstarch mixture, stirring to combine.
3. Continue to cook until thick. Turn off heat and allow to cool.
4. Chill overnight, or for at least 10 hours.

Quick Fruit Sauce

Makes ½ cup, serves 4

1 8-oz jar jam

1. Puree jam in food processor, adding 1 tsp of water as needed to achieve a thick, syrupy consistency.

NUTRITIONAL INFORMATION

BLUEBERRY SAUCE (PER 2 TBSP SERVING) (USING 1 TBSP AGAVE)
Calories **31**; Calories from Fat **1**; Total Fat **0.1g**; Cholesterol **0mg**; Total Carbohydrate **8.2g**; Dietary Fiber **1.1g**; Sugars **6.2g**; Protein **0.3g**

QUICK FRUIT SAUCE (PER 2 TBSP SERVING) Calories **79**; Calories from Fat **0**; Total Fat **0.0g**; Cholesterol **0mg**; Total Carbohydrate **19.5g**; Sugars **13.8g**; Protein **0.1g**

Dips, Snacks, & Finger Foods

Mexican Dip

Makes 2 cups | This dip reminds me of all those cheesy and rich Mexican dips you find at parties, except this one is made from beans and doesn't have any fat or cholesterol.

1 15-oz can cannellini beans, drained and rinsed
1 red bell pepper, seeded and top removed
1 tbsp chili powder
1 tbsp onion flakes
1½ tsp ground cumin
¼ tsp fine salt
¼ tsp pepper
dash of granulated garlic powder
dash of paprika
juice of ½ lime
⅓ c nutritional yeast
⅔ c (or less) salsa
1 jalapeño, seeded (optional)
½ c canned or cooked black beans

1. Preheat oven to 350°F.
2. Grease an 8-inch round or 9-inch square casserole dish and set aside.
3. Add all ingredients except black beans to a food processor.
4. Blend until smooth and transfer mixture to prepared casserole dish.
5. Gently stir in black beans and bake for 30 to 40 minutes, or until dip is thoroughly warm.

VARIATION

Spicy Nacho Dip 🅖 🆂 ➷ Add cayenne pepper to taste and swirl hot sauce into the dip after baking

CHEF'S NOTE: *Garnish with diced tomatoes, chopped green onions, and lettuce if desired.*

NUTRITIONAL INFORMATION (PER ¼-CUP SERVING) ➷ Calories **80**; Calories From Fat **8**; Total Fat **0.9g**; Cholesterol **0mg**; Total Carbohydrate **13.8g**; Dietary Fiber **4.4g**; Sugars **2.1g**; Protein **5.1g**

Low-Fat Guacamole

Makes 2 cups | *Pictured on pg. 228* | More appropriately called "edamole," this dip is a guacamole knock-off. The texture is a little different and it doesn't taste the same as guacamole—but it's close. I've even managed to fool a few friends and my husband with this recipe. Serve it with baked corn chips or slather it into a burrito.

2 c frozen edamame or
  peas, thawed
¼ c fresh cilantro
1 garlic clove
½ small sweet onion (or 1 to
  2 tbsp dried onion flakes)
1 tsp ground cumin
juice of 2 small limes
sea salt, to taste
cayenne powder, to taste
1 salad tomato, diced

1. Combine all ingredients except tomato in a food processor and blend until smooth, stopping and scraping the sides as necessary.

2. If the dip is too rustic, add 1 to 2 tbsp of water.

3. Stir in tomatoes and serve.

> CHEF'S NOTE: *For a more authentic representation of guacamole or a higher-fat version, add 2 to 4 tbsp of fresh avocado and a few drops of Vegan Worcheshire Sauce (pg. 272).*

NUTRITIONAL INFORMATION (PER 2 TBSP SERVING) Calories **25**;
Calories from Fat **10**; Total Fat **1.1g**; Cholesterol **0mg**; Total Carbohydrate **2.2g**; Dietary Fiber **0.7g**;
Protein **2.1g**

Ranch Dip

Makes 1 cup | *Pictured opposite* | This easy recipe is designed with raw veggies in mind. Great for carrots, celery, broccoli, and cauliflower dipping.

1 c Mayo (pg. 271)
½ tsp granulated garlic
   powder
½ tsp granulated onion
   powder
salt, to taste
1 tbsp fresh minced parsley
1 to 2 tsp fresh minced dill

1. Combine Mayo, garlic powder, onion powder, and a pinch of salt in a small bowl, stirring to combine.
2. Stir in fresh parsley and dill and mix until well incorporated.
3. Taste and add more salt or garlic if necessary or desired.
4. Chill until serving.

NUTRITIONAL INFORMATION (PER 1 TBSP SERVING) Calories **10**; Calories from Fat **2**; Total Fat **0.2g**; Cholesterol **0mg**; Total Carbohydrate **0.5g**; Protein **1.6g**

Ultimate 7-Layer Dip G 😀 ✪

Serves 10 | *Pictured opposite* | This is the ultimate party dip! Serve with baked corn chips.

1 15-oz can vegetarian
   refried beans
1 to 1½ cup Low-Fat
   Guacamole (pg. 231)
Bacon Bits (pg. 137)
Nacho Cheese Sauce
   (pg. 265) or Quick Queso
   Sauce (pg. 263)
1 4-oz can diced black
   olives, drained
1 c mild salsa or 2 tomatoes,
   diced
Sour Cream (pg. 271)
fresh cilantro or lettuce,
   chopped

1. Transfer refried beans to a 9-inch square dish and spread around to make a bottom layer.

2. Add Low-Fat Guacamole over top, followed by Bacon Bits and then the Quick Queso or Nacho Cheese Sauce.

3. Sprinkle olives and tomatoes on top. Or, if using salsa, spoon it into the center, on top of the dip.

4. Garnish with a few dollops of Sour Cream and freshly chopped cilantro or lettuce.

CHEF'S NOTE: *You can also mix the taco seasonings from the Blue Corn Chickpea Tacos (pg. 97) with leftover Sour Cream (pg. 271) to make another delicious dip layer (as pictured).*

NUTRITIONAL INFORMATION 🍫 Calories **161.6**; Calories from Fat **37.3**; Total Fat **4.1g**; Cholesterol **0mg**; Total Carbohydrate **20.3g**; Dietary Fiber **5.6g**; Sugars **3.9g**; Protein **11.8g**

Chili-Lime Corn Chips

Serves 4 | *Pictured opposite* | These chips pair well with salsa or black bean dip, but are also great individually as a snack or used for scooping up the Chili sans Carne (pg. 81).

1 small lime, washed
1 10-oz package 8-inch corn
   tortillas
½ tsp chili powder
½ tsp fine salt
¼ tsp granulated garlic
   powder (optional)

1. Preheat toaster oven to 350°F (conventional oven to 325°F).
2. Grease a cookie sheet or toaster oven tray and set aside.
3. Zest lime and reserve lime for juice later.
4. Using a pizza cutter, slice each tortilla into 6 triangles.
5. Transfer chips to a bowl, spray with cooking spray, and add lime zest, chili powder, salt, and garlic powder, if using.
6. Using your hands, toss to coat.
7. Re-spray and toss a second time, making sure all of the chips are lightly covered with zest and spices.
8. Place chips on cookie sheet or tray in a single layer and bake for 5 minutes; flip and bake for 5 to 7 minutes more, until crisp.
9. Allow chips to cool for 5 to 10 minutes, allowing them to crisp up a bit more.
10. Squeeze fresh lime juice over top before serving.

VARIATION

Chipotle-Lime Corn Chips   Replace chili powder with ¼ tsp of chipotle powder.

NUTRITIONAL INFORMATION Calories **44.3**; Calories from Fat **4.6**; Total Fat **0.5g**; Cholesterol **0mg**; Total Carbohydrate **9.4g**; Dietary Fiber **1.1g**; Sugars **0g**; Protein **1.1g**

Cinnamon-Sugar Tortilla Chips

Serves 2 | Back in the '80s Taco Bell sold triangular cinnamon-sugar tortilla chips that I just loved. Then they switched to cinnamon-sugar twists, which leave much to be desired in the nutrition department. Here's my healthy version of their original snack. Careful, they're addictive!

2 tsp raw sugar
4 whole-wheat tortillas
½ tsp ground cinnamon
ground ginger to taste,
    about ⅛ to ¼ tsp

1. Preheat toaster oven to 350°F (convention oven to 325°F).

2. Grease a cookie sheet or toaster oven tray and set aside.

3. Grind sugar down into a finer consistency.

4. Using a pizza cutter, slice each tortilla into 6 to 8 triangles.

5. Transfer to a bowl and spray with cooking spray; add sugar, cinnamon, and a light dash of ginger, or to taste.

6. Toss chips with your hands to coat.

7. Re-spray and toss a second time, making sure all of the chips are lightly covered in sugar and spices.

8. Place chips on cookie sheet or tray in a single layer and bake for 5 minutes.

9. Flip chips over and bake for 5 to 7 minutes more, until crisp.

10. Let chips cool for 5 to 10 minutes, allowing them to crisp up a bit more.

NUTRITIONAL INFORMATION 🥄 Calories **79.4**; Calories from Fat **14.8**; Total Fat **1.6g**; Cholesterol **0mg**; Total Carbohydrate **14g**; Fiber **0.8g**; Sugars **0.7g**; Protein **0.1g**

Crispy Tortilla Sticks

Makes 1 cup, about 4 servings | Great on top of soups, slipped into the BBQ Chop Wrap (pg. 91), or munched on as a snack. These sticks are also used in the Tortilla Soup (pg. 68).

4 6-inch corn tortillas

1. Preheat toaster oven to 350°F (conventional oven to 325°F).
2. Grease a cookie sheet or toaster oven tray and set aside.
3. Cut tortillas in half crosswise, then into ⅛-inch-wide strips, about the width of a matchstick.
4. Transfer to a bowl, spray with cooking spray, and toss to coat.
5. Repeat a second time, making sure all of the strips are lightly covered.
6. Place on the cookie sheet or tray in a single layer and bake for 5 minutes, until crispy.
7. Let cool for 5 to 10 minutes, allowing them to crisp up a bit more.

NUTRITIONAL INFORMATION 🥄 Calories **42.3**; Calories from Fat **4.3**; Fat **0.5g**; Cholesterol **0mg**; Protein **1.2g**; Carbohydrate **8.9g**; Fiber **1g**; Sugar **0g**

Fruity Cereal Bars

Makes 9 squares | *Pictured opposite* | A truly whole-grain and vegan imitation of commercial breakfast cereal bars.

1 c rolled oats
1 c whole-wheat pastry
    flour
½ tsp baking powder
½ tsp fine salt
½ c raw sugar
½ c applesauce
¼ c non-dairy milk
1 tbsp agave nectar
1 tsp vanilla extract
7 oz jam, any flavor

CHEF'S NOTE:
*For a more cake-like
batter, try using
instant oats.*

1. Preheat oven to 350F.

2. In a medium bowl, whisk oats, flour, baking powder, and salt together, then add sugar, applesauce, non-dairy milk, agave, and vanilla, stirring to combine.

3. Grab a large piece of parchment paper, enough that it lines a 9-inch baking dish with enough paper excess on the sides to work as a handle when you pull the paper out.

4. Divide the batter in half, spreading half on the paper to form a layer.

5. Lift paper with batter out and set aside. Then grease pan and pour remaining batter in, spreading around to form a layer; set aside.

6. Whiz jam with 1 tbsp of water to make a filling, then spread on to batter evenly.

7. Carefully but quickly flip the remaining batter out on top of the jam, pat down gently and bake for 25 to 30 minutes, or until light brown and no longer wet to the touch.

8. Allow to cool completely before cutting slices. Transfer slices to a wire cooling wrack to prevent bottoms from becoming soft.

NUTRITIONAL INFORMATION ⬥ Calories **204**; Calories from Fat **8**; Total Fat **0.9g**; Cholesterol **0mg**; Total Carbohydrate **45.9g**; Dietary Fiber **2.8g**; Sugars **25.1g**; Protein **2.8g**

Mini-Cheese Pizzas

Makes 8 mini-pizzas | *Pictured opposite* | This is my quick and easy pizza recipe that's fat-free and really tasty. The cheese sauce doesn't taste like mozzarella or dairy cheese per se, but it's delicious on pizza and a wonderful substitute. Feel free to use regular pizza dough or 4 regular whole-wheat pitas if you prefer.

½ c pizza sauce
8 whole-wheat mini-pitas
1 c non-dairy milk
¼ c nutritional yeast
2 tbsp cornstarch
2 tbsp whole-wheat pastry
    flour
3 tsp lemon juice
2 tsp yellow miso
1 tsp granulated onion
    powder
½ tsp granulated garlic
    powder
¼ tsp dry mustard powder

1. Preheat toaster oven to 450°F (conventional oven to 425°F).

2. Spoon 1 tbsp of pizza sauce on each pita (2 tbsp if using regular pitas).

3. Use the back of a spoon to spread a thin layer of sauce around each pita evenly and set aside.

4. Whisk all remaining ingredients together in a saucepan.

5. Heat on high heat until bubbling.

6. Reduce heat to medium and allow sauce to thicken, stirring constantly.

7. Spoon over prepared pizza and bake for 4 to 7 minutes, until pita is warm and slightly crisp, and cheese has melted and formed a skin on top.

8. Let cool for 3 to 5 minutes before eating.

> **CHEF'S NOTE:** *Gluten-free flours and blends may be substituted for the whole-wheat pasty flour.*

NUTRITIONAL INFORMATION 🍽 Calories **43**; Calories from Fat **5**; Total Fat **0.6g**; Cholesterol **0mg**; Total Carbohydrate **7.5g**; Dietary Fiber **1.1g**; Sugars **1.6g**; Protein **2.2g**

Loaded Nachos

Serves 4 | *Pictured opposite* | These nachos will knock your socks off. They're so freakin' good you'll deny they're healthy. If you can't find roasted corn, frozen yellow corn is a fine substitution.

2 large tomatoes
1 bunch green onions
1 to 2 9-oz bags baked corn chips
1½ c canned or cooked black beans
1 cup frozen roasted corn, thawed
1 4-oz can sliced black olives, drained
1 5-oz can sliced jalapeños, drained
1 recipe Nacho Cheese Sauce (pg. 265), warm
¼ c Sour Cream (pg. 271; optional)

1. Seed and dice tomatoes and set aside.
2. Slice green onions on the diagonal, reserving green parts only.
3. Fill your serving bowl halfway with baked corn chips.
4. Add half of the beans and corn.
5. Add more chips on top, followed by the remainder of the black beans and corn.
6. Add olives, jalapeños, and half of the tomatoes, then pour Nacho Cheese Sauce over top.
7. Garnish with remaining tomatoes, green onions, and a few dollops of Sour Cream, if using.

NUTRITIONAL INFORMATION 🥄 Calories **248**; Calories from Fat **53**; Total Fat **5.9g**; Cholesterol **0mg**; Total Carbohydrate **39.8g**; Dietary Fiber **11.2g**; Sugars **7.8g**; Protein **13.1g**

Cha-Cha Chili Nachos

Serves 4 | Leftover Chili sans Carne (pg. 81) is awesome on a pile of corn chips and served with fresh jalapeños, onions, and spicy salsa. For a more traditional nachos experience, add Quick Queso Sauce (pg. 263), Cheddar Cheesy Sauce (pg. 264), or Nacho Cheese Sauce (pg. 265).

baked corn chips
1½ c Chili sans Carne
   (pg. 81)
1 small sweet onion, diced
1 4-oz can sliced jalapeños
¼ c Sour Cream
   (pg. 271; optional)
¼ c spicy salsa (optional)

1. Fill a big serving bowl with chips and spoon warm chili over top.
2. Then add onion and jalapeños followed by dollops of Sour Cream and spicy salsa, if using.

NUTRITIONAL INFORMATION ☞ Calories **104.8**; Calories from Fat **6.8**; Total Fat **0.7g**; Cholesterol **0mg**; Total Carbohydrate **17.9g**; Dietary Fiber **5g**; Sugars **3.4g**; Protein **7.6g**

Bean Cakes

Makes 16 cakes | These bean cakes will dazzle anyone who tries them. Make them for a fun and tasty weeknight meal or dress them up as hors d'oeuvres at your next dinner party. Top them with fresh julienned vegetables, chunky salsa, or a complementary spread.

1 15-oz can refried
    black beans
½ c Breadcrumbs (pg. 284)
1 tbsp yellow cornmeal
1 tsp chili powder
¼ tsp ground cumin
1 tsp lime zest

1. Preheat oven to 350°F.
2. Grease cookie sheet or line with parchment paper.
3. Mix all ingredients together by hand.
4. Add an extra 1 tbsp of cornmeal if it is too sticky to work with, or refrigerate 5 to 10 minutes.
5. Lightly flour hands and pick off a portion of the mixture and roll into a walnut-sized ball.
6. Place it on the cookie sheet and flatten into a patty with the palm of your hand.
7. Repeat with the rest of the mixture.
8. Spray with cooking oil and bake for 15 minutes or until firm.

NUTRITIONAL INFORMATION (APPROX. 2 CAKES) 🍪 Calories **24**; Calories from Fat **3**; Total Fat **0.3g**; Cholesterol **0mg**; Total Carbohydrate **4.2g**; Dietary Fiber **0.8g**; Protein **1.2g**

Corncakes

Makes 8 cakes | These cakes are a cross between cornbread and pancakes. They're a great alternative to pancakes at brunch or as a light appetizer when made into a mini-pancake size. Serve with Low-Fat Guacamole (pg. 231), salsa, or diced cremini mushrooms and red bell peppers cooked in a little water and garnished with fresh cilantro.

2 tbsp pure maple syrup
1 tbsp lemon juice
1 c non-dairy milk
½ c yellow cornmeal
½ c whole-wheat pastry flour
½ tsp baking powder
¼ tsp baking soda
¼ tsp fine salt
2 tsp Cajun Essence (pg. 274)

1. Combine the maple and lemon with non-dairy milk in your measuring cup and whisk to combine; set aside.

2. In a mixing bowl, whisk remaining dry ingredients together, then pour in wet mixture, stirring to combine.

3. If you have time, cover and let set in fridge for 10 minutes.

4. Cook as you would pancakes, pouring about ¼ cup of batter onto a sprayed nonstick skillet.

5. Cook the first side for 5 to 7 minutes, then flip and cook for another 2 to 3 minutes on the second side, but be careful not to burn.

NUTRITIONAL INFORMATION 🥄 Calories **78**; Calories from Fat **6**; Total Fat **0.7g**; Cholesterol **0mg**; Total Carbohydrate **16.0g**; Dietary Fiber **1.5g**; Sugars **3.8g**; Protein **2.1g**

Spreads, Gravies, & Sauces

Nutty Spread ⬛ Ⓖ Ⓢ 😀 ★

Makes 1 cup | *Pictured opposite and on pg. 250* | This is my low-fat alternative to plain peanut butter. It's perfect for spreading on toast and crackers or as a dip with fresh apple slices. Pure maple syrup may be substituted for the agave nectar.

1 c cooked navy or
    cannellini beans
¼ c smooth peanut butter
2 tbsp agave nectar
¼ tsp ground cinnamon
salt, as needed

1. If peanut butter was refrigerated, let warm to room temperature first.

2. Combine all ingredients except salt in a processor and let the motor run until the mixture is somewhat smooth and there are no visible traces of the beans left.

3. Taste; if it's still too beany, add 1 tbsp of smooth peanut butter.

4. If you used unsalted peanut butter, you may want to add ¼ to ¾ tsp of fine salt. Likewise, if you used unsweetened peanut butter, consider adding an additional 1 tsp of agave. Store leftovers in an airtight container.

CHEF'S NOTE: *Other smooth nut butters such as almond, cashew, and soy nut may be substituted.*

NUTRITIONAL INFORMATION (PER 2 TBSP SERVING) 🥄 Calories **90**;
Calories from Fat **37**; Total Fat **4.1g**; Saturated Fat **0.8g**; Cholesterol **0mg**; Total Carbohydrate **10.6g**;
Dietary Fiber **2.5g**; Sugars **4.5g**; Protein **3.8g**

Brown Gravy

Makes 2 cups | When I realized most brown gravies aren't vegetarian I set out to make my own healthy version. Serve it with Dirty Mashed Potatoes (pg. 190), Hippie Loaf (pg. 144), and French fries. Yes, I eat my French fries with gravy; it's a Scranton thing. Try it!

¼ c nutritional yeast
¼ c whole-wheat pastry
    flour or other flour
2 c vegetable broth
2 tbsp low-sodium soy
    sauce
a few dashes of pepper
1 tsp granulated onion
    powder
½ tsp granulated garlic
    powder
salt, to taste

1. In a small nonstick skillet, whisk nutritional yeast and flour together and toast over medium heat until it smells toasty, about 4 minutes.

2. Transfer to a medium saucepan and whisk in remaining ingredients except the salt.

3. Bring to a boil and allow sauce to thicken as desired and add salt. For an even thicker gravy, mix 1 tbsp of cornstarch with 2 tbsp of water and pour it into the gravy.

No-Beef Gravy

Makes 1 cup | *Pictured on pg. 132* | Designed to complement the Seitan Pot Roast (pg. 132), this gravy has a rich, beef-like flavor with a subtle hint of ginger. Fresh or dried herbs such as thyme can also be added for a more complex flavor.

1 c No-Beef Broth (pg. 279)
1 tbsp cornstarch
1 tbsp whole-wheat flour or
    other flour
salt, to taste
pepper, to taste

1. Whisk broth, cornstarch, and flour together until well combined.

2. Bring to a boil over medium heat and allow to thicken slightly.

3. Add salt and pepper.

NUTRITIONAL INFORMATION

BROWN GRAVY (PER 1/4-CUP SERVING) Calories **28**; Calories from Fat **1**;
Total Fat **0.1g**; Cholesterol **0mg**; Total Carbohydrate **5.4g**; Dietary Fiber **0.8g**; Protein **1.4g**

NO-BEEF GRAVY (PER 1/4-CUP SERVING) Calories **21.3**; Calories from Fat **0.8**;
Total Fat **0.1g**; Cholesterol **0mg**; Total Carbohydrate **4.3g**; Dietary Fiber **0.53g**; Sugars **0.2g**; Protein **0.9g**

Thanksgiving Gravy

Makes 1 cup | Designed to be the perfect complement to Torkey (Tofu Turkey) (pg. 152) and Dirty Mashed Potatoes (pg. 190), this gravy is thick and heavenly.

¼ c nutritional yeast
¼ c whole-wheat pastry
   flour or other
1 c non-dairy milk
1 small onion, diced
8 oz white mushrooms,
   thinly sliced
2 tbsp soy sauce
1 tsp rubbed sage (not
   powdered)
1 tsp dried thyme
salt, to taste
pepper, to taste

1. Whisk nutritional yeast and flour together with non-dairy milk and set aside.

2. Line a large frying pan with a thin layer of water and cook onion and mushrooms over high heat until the mushrooms start to soften and turn brown and most of the water has evaporated.

3. Add non-dairy milk mixture, soy sauce, and herbs, stirring to combine.

4. Bring to a boil and continue to cook until thick.

5. Add salt and pepper.

Sausage Gravy

Makes 2½ cups | Perfect for drenching over Biscuits (pg. 38).

2 c non-dairy milk
¼ c whole-wheat pastry
   flour or other
⅛ c vegan sausage,
   crumbled
pepper, to taste

1. Whisk non-dairy milk and flour together.

2. Add to a saucepan and heat over medium.

3. Add in sausage and bring to a boil over high heat, then reduce heat to medium.

4. Allow gravy to thicken to a desired consistency.

5. Add pepper (I like it really peppery!) to taste.

NUTRITIONAL INFORMATION

THANKSGIVING GRAVY (PER 1/4-CUP SERVING) Calories **70**; Calories from Fat **9**; Total Fat **1.0g**; Cholesterol **0mg**; Total Carbohydrate **10.9g**; Dietary Fiber **2.6g**; Sugars **3.3g**; Protein **6.1g**

SAUSAGE GRAVY (PER 1/4-CUP SERVING, NOT INCLUDING VEGAN MEAT) Calories **38**; Calories from Fat **8**; Total Fat **0.2g**; Cholesterol **0mg**; Total Carbohydrate **5.5g**; Sugars **2.0g**; Protein **1.9g**

Southern-Style BBQ Sauce

Serves 4 | Until I lived in South Carolina, I had no idea there was more than one type of barbecue sauce. Turns out there are three: ketchup-based, mustard-based, and vinegar-based. South Carolinians make it with mustard, and boy is it good.

⅔ c prepared yellow mustard

¼ c brown sugar

2 tbsp cornstarch

2 tbsp pure maple syrup, or to taste

1 tbsp soy sauce

½ tsp granulated garlic powder

½ tsp paprika

¼ tsp Vegan Worcestershire sauce (pg. 272; optional)

⅛ tsp cayenne powder, or to taste

1. Whisk all ingredients together with ½ cup of water and bring to a boil over medium-high heat.

2. Allow mixture to thicken to the consistency of a salad dressing, or to desired thickness. Stir as needed.

3. Taste, adding more sugar or maple syrup as desired.

4. Store leftovers in an airtight container in the fridge for up to 1 week.

> **CHEF'S NOTE:** *Smother Basic Baked Tofu (pg. 138) and cooked tempeh in this sauce for some vegan-style Southern barbecue, or drizzle sauce over fresh corn or blanched greens.*

NUTRITIONAL INFORMATION (PER ¼-CUP SERVING) Calories **108**; Calories from Fat **15**; Total Fat **1.7g**; Cholesterol **0mg**; Total Carbohydrate **22.2g**; Dietary Fiber **1.6g**; Sugars **15.3g**; Protein **2.2g**

Creole Roasted Red-Pepper Sauce

Makes 1 cup | *Pictured on pg. 120* | This Cajun-inspired sauce is the perfect complement to the Cajun Meatloaf (pg. 141) but also jazzes up cooked brown rice and steamed greens.

½ c chopped onion
1 c vegetable broth
1 8-oz jar roasted red
   peppers in water,
   drained
¼ tsp Cajun Essence
   (pg. 274), or to taste
2 bay leaves
⅛ tsp liquid smoke
hot sauce as desired
salt, to taste
white pepper, to taste

1. Cook onion over medium heat in ¼ cup of broth until translucent, about 2 minutes.

2. Transfer to a blender, add red bell peppers, and blend until smooth.

3. Return to saucepan and add broth, Cajun Essence, bay leaves, and liquid smoke and bring to a boil.

4. Once it's boiling, reduce heat to low and simmer until thoroughly warm, about 5 minutes.

5. Fish out bay leaves and add hot sauce, salt, and white pepper.

CHEF'S NOTE: *For a more authentic sauce, add 1 celery stalk, diced, and 1 large carrot, peeled and diced, with the onions to complete the holy trinity. You may also substitute 1¼ cups of diced canned tomatoes for the red bell peppers.*

NUTRITIONAL INFORMATION (PER ¼-CUP SERVING) Calories **22**; Calories from Fat **1**; Total Fat **0.1g**; Cholesterol **0mg**; Total Carbohydrate **5.1g**; Dietary Fiber **0.9g**; Sugars **3.1g**; Protein **0.7g**

Quick Marinara Sauce

Makes 3 cups | My best friend Jim turned me on to making my own marinara sauce. He kept insisting it was easier, cheaper, and a lot healthier than any store bought variety, so finally I tried it, and *wow*! It's so easy it's ridiculous!

1 28-oz can crushed tomatoes, with basil

2 tbsp Italian seasoning

½ tsp granulated garlic powder

1 tsp granulated onion powder

¼ tsp red pepper flakes, or to taste (optional)

1 tsp agave nectar (optional)

1. Combine tomatoes and seasonings in a saucepan over medium heat.

2. Bring to a near boil and reduce heat to medium, continuing to cook for 3 minutes and stirring occasionally.

3. Taste; if too acidic add agave and more red pepper flakes, if desired.

4. Continue to simmer over low heat for 10 to 20 minutes, until the herbs lose their raw taste and the sauce is thoroughly warmed.

NUTRITIONAL INFORMATION (PER ¼-CUP SERVING) Calories **35**; Calories from Fat **6**; Total Fat **0.7g**; Cholesterol **0mg**; Total Carbohydrate **5.8g**; Dietary Fiber **2.1g**; Sugars **4.0g**; Protein **1.6g**

Enchilada Sauce

Makes 4 cups | *Pictured opposite* | The secret to making authentic enchilada sauce is the addition of cocoa. Once you've had homemade you'll never buy enchilada sauce in a can again. It's easy to make, inexpensive, and really tasty when you do it yourself.

2 tbsp whole-wheat pastry flour or other flour
1 tsp unsweetened cocoa
2 tbsp chili powder
1 tsp dried marjoram or oregano
1 tsp ground cumin
½ tsp granulated garlic powder
2 c vegetable broth
1 8-oz can tomato sauce
salt, to taste (optional)

1. Whisk flour, cocoa, and spices together in a saucepan without turning on the heat.
2. Add ¼ cup of broth and stir into a paste.
3. Slowly whisk in remaining broth and an additional cup of water.
4. Bring to a boil over medium heat and whisk in tomato sauce.
5. Allow to cook a few minutes and thicken slightly to the consistency of tomato soup.
6. Remove from heat and add salt if necessary.

NUTRITIONAL INFORMATION (PER ¼-CUP SERVING) Calories **13**; Calories from Fat **2**; Total Fat **0.3g**; Cholesterol **0mg**; Total Carbohydrate **2.8g**; Dietary Fiber **0.7g**; Sugars **0.8g**; Protein **0.5g**

Quick Queso Sauce

Makes 1 cup | *Pictured opposite* | It's okay to go at this sauce with a spoon. I won't judge. It's also great with nachos, burritos, enchiladas, or inside a black bean quesadilla.

1 c non-dairy milk
⅓ c nutritional yeast
2 tbsp whole-wheat flour
1 tsp granulated onion powder
½ tsp granulated garlic powder
½ tsp ground cumin
¼ tsp paprika
¼ tsp chili powder or cayenne (optional)
¼ tsp salt, or to taste

1. Whisk all ingredients together in a saucepan.
2. Bring to a boil over medium heat, stirring often until thick.
3. Serve immediately.

VARIATION
Quick Mexican Queso Sauce Add 1 10-oz can of Rotel tomatoes with green chilies; leave chunky or puree in a blender before heating.

> **CHEF'S NOTE:**
> *A gluten-free flour or blend may be substituted for the whole-wheat flour.*

NUTRITIONAL INFORMATION

QUICK QUESO SAUCE (PER 1/4-CUP SERVING) Calories **45**; Calories from Fat **7**; Total Fat **0.8g**; Cholesterol **0mg**; Total Carbohydrate **6.2g**; Dietary Fiber **1.6g**; Sugars **1.8g**; Protein **4.0g**

MEXICAN QUESO SAUCE (PER 1/4-CUP SERVING) Calories **57**; Calories from Fat **7**; Total Fat **0.8g**; Cholesterol **0mg**; Total Carbohydrate **8.5g**; Dietary Fiber **2.2g**; Sugars **3.5g**; Protein **4.6g**

Cheddar Cheesy Sauce

Makes 1 cup | *Pictured on pg. 158* | This is my favorite cheese sauce recipe. It's perfect on pasta when you're in the mood for mac 'n' cheese, but it's also fantastic over potatoes au gratin or steamed vegetables. One night, when my fridge was lookin' pretty empty, I poured this sauce over sweet potato slices and vegan chorizo, baked it, and ended up with one awesome casserole.

1¼ c non-dairy milk
⅓ c nutritional yeast
2 tbsp yellow miso
2 tbsp cornstarch
1 tsp granulated onion
    powder
1 tsp granulated garlic
    powder
½ tsp paprika
¼ tsp turmeric

1 Whisk all ingredients together in a saucepan.

2 Bring to a boil over medium heat, then reduce heat to low, stirring frequently until it thickens slightly.

NUTRITIONAL INFORMATION (PER ¼-CUP SERVING) Calories **67**; Calories from Fat **12**; Total Fat **1.4g**; Cholesterol **0mg**; Total Carbohydrate **9.4g**; Dietary Fiber **2.0g**; Sugars **2.8g**; Protein **5.1g**

Nacho Cheese Sauce

Makes 1 cup | *Pictured on pg. 244* | If you love the low-fat nacho cheese recipe on my website, Happyherbivore.com, you're in for a real treat with this fat-free sister version. It's still rich and cheesy like the original recipe but slightly spicier and ultra-healthy.

1 c non-dairy milk
⅓ c nutritional yeast
3 tbsp rolled oats
½ tsp granulated onion
    powder
½ tsp ground cumin
¼ c mild salsa
2 tsp yellow miso
2 tsp cornstarch
1 tsp lemon juice (optional)

1. Combine all ingredients into a food processor or blender and whiz until smooth and mostly homogenous.

2. Transfer to a saucepan and cook over medium heat, stirring frequently until it's thick and cheesy.

3. Taste, adding lemon if desired.

> **CHEF'S NOTE:** *¼-cup of roasted red bell pepper can be substituted for the salsa.*

NUTRITIONAL INFORMATION (PER ¼-CUP SERVING) Calories **64**; Calories from Fat **11**; Total Fat **1.2g**; Cholesterol **0mg**; Total Carbohydrate **9.4g**; Dietary Fiber **1.9g**; Sugars **2.3g**; Protein **4.6g**

Tofu Ricotta Cheese

Makes 3 cups | Quick and easy, this protein-packed ricotta goes beautifully on pizza or salads, or tossed with pasta.

1 lb extra-firm tofu, drained
1 tsp lemon juice
¼ c nutritional yeast
2 tbsp Italian seasoning
¼ tsp granulated garlic
    powder
salt, to taste
pepper, to taste

1. Wrap the tofu in a clean kitchen cloth and place between two cutting boards.

2. Place a large, heavy object on the top board.

3. Allow to rest for 20 minutes, forcing excess water out of the tofu.

4. Crumble tofu with your hands so it's broken down into smaller pieces but not yet the consistency of ricotta.

5. Mix in lemon juice, nutritional yeast, Italian seasoning, and garlic powder, plus salt and pepper.

6. Incorporate all ingredients with your hands, breaking down tofu to the consistency of ricotta or feta cheese as you mix it together.

NUTRITIONAL INFORMATION (PER ¼-CUP SERVING) Calories **137**; Calories from Fat **66**; Total Fat **2.4g**; Cholesterol **0mg**; Total Carbohydrate **7.5g**; Dietary Fiber **3.6g**; Sugars **1.4g**; Protein **13g**

Cranberry Sauce

Makes 2 cups | I like my cranberry sauce slightly sweet and still a little tart. It's the prefect addition to any holiday meal, but I really love eating it splattered over Basic Baked Tofu (pg. 138).

2½ c fresh cranberries
¼ c agave nectar, or to taste
¼ c fresh orange juice
    (optional)

1. Combine cranberries, 1 cup of water, and agave and bring to a boil.

2. Continue to boil for 10 to 20 minutes, adding orange juice, if using, after the first 10 minutes of cooking.

3. Once most of the cranberries have popped and the sauce has thickened, turn off heat and cool to room temperature.

4. Transfer to a container and refrigerate overnight, or at least 4 hours before serving.

NUTRITIONAL INFORMATION (PER ¼-CUP SERVING) Calories **22**; Calories from Fat **0**; Total Fat **0.0g**; Cholesterol **0mg**; Total Carbohydrate **5.8g**; Dietary Fiber **0.9g**; Sugars **4.3g**; Protein **0.1g**

Condiments, Spices, & More

Mayo

Makes 1 cup | Nasoya makes a fat-free vegan mayonnaise and some generic low-fat mayos are accidentally vegan. Still, they can be hard to find, so here is an easy and inexpensive recipe for making your own low-fat vegan mayo at home.

1 12.3-oz package Mori-Nu tofu
2 to 3 tbsp Dijon mustard
2 tsp distilled white vinegar
lemon juice, to taste
agave nectar, to taste

1. In a blender or small food processor, blend tofu with Dijon and vinegar until smooth and creamy.
2. Add a few drops of lemon juice and a few drops of agave nectar and blend again.
3. Taste and add more lemon, agave, or Dijon as needed or desired. Chill until you're ready to use.

Sour Cream

Makes 1 cup | Quick and easy to make with a fraction of the fat compared to dairy and commercial cream cheeses.

1 12.3-oz package Mori-Nu firm tofu
2 to 4 tbsp lemon juice
½ tsp distilled white vinegar
⅛ tsp fine salt
1 tsp dry mustard powder
agave nectar, to taste
light dash granulated garlic powder
1 tsp dried or fresh dill (optional)

1. Combine tofu with 2 tbsp of lemon juice, vinegar, a pinch of salt, mustard powder, a few drops of agave, and a light dash of garlic powder and blend until smooth and creamy.
2. Taste and add more lemon and/or sweetener if necessary or desired. Stir in dill before serving if using.

VARIATION
Lime Crème 🍲 🄵 🄶 ⟿ Use lime juice instead of lemon juice and add 1½ tbsp of chopped fresh cilantro.

NUTRITIONAL INFORMATION

MAYO (PER 1-TBSP SERVING) ⟿ Calories **9**; Calories from Fat **2**; Total Fat **0.2g**; Cholesterol **0mg**; Total Carbohydrate **0.3g**; Protein **1.6g**

SOUR CREAM (PER 1-TBSP SERVING) (WITH 1 TBSP AGAVE) ⟿ Calories **13**; Calories from Fat **2**; Total Fat **0.2g**; Cholesterol **0mg**; Total Carbohydrate **1.4g**; Sugars **1.1g**; Protein **1.6g**

Vegan Worcestershire Sauce

Makes 1 cup | Most commercial Worcestershire sauces contain anchovies, although there are a few vegetarian brands on the market. While nothing beats the ease of bottled sauce, this DIY recipe is allergen-free and very inexpensive to make. Worcestershire sauce is traditionally used as a condiment for meat, and consequently is a great marinade for veggie burgers and acts as a flavoring agent in many meat substitute recipes.

6 tbsp apple cider vinegar
2 tbsp tamari
1 tbsp brown sugar or 1 tsp molasses
2 tsp prepared mustard (any)
¼ tsp granulated onion powder
¼ tsp granulated garlic powder
¼ tsp ground ginger
⅛ tsp ground cinnamon
light dash of cayenne pepper or chili powder
light dash of allspice or ground cloves
salt (optional)

1. Whisk all ingredients together with ¼ cup of water until well combined.
2. Add salt if desired.
3. Store in an airtight container in the fridge.

> **CHEF'S NOTE:** *Soy sauce may be substituted for the tamari.*

NUTRITIONAL INFORMATION (Per 1 tsp serving) Calories **2**; Calories from Fat **0**; Total Fat **0.0g**; Cholesterol **0mg**; Total Carbohydrate **0.4g**; Protein **0.1g**

Poultry Seasoning Mix

Makes ¼ cup | This savory herb mixture is my favorite seasoning. It's traditionally used for seasoning poultry, which is why it's key in creating Chicken-Style Seitan (pg. 142) and Torkey (Tofu Turkey) (pg. 152).

1 tbsp dried rosemary
1 tbsp dried thyme
1 tbsp rubbed sage (not powdered)
1 tbsp dried marjoram or oregano
1 tbsp dried parsley or basil

1. Grind herbs together in a mortar and pestle until coarse like the consistency of sea salt, but not powdered.
2. Store in an airtight container.

> **CHEF'S NOTE:** *If you can find granulated, not powdered, poultry seasoning that isn't a rub, feel free to use it instead for convenience instead of blending your own. I like Cost Plus World Market's generic brand.*

NUTRITIONAL INFORMATION ⬥ (Per 1 tbsp serving) Calories **10**; Calories from Fat **3**; Total Fat **0.4g**; Cholesterol **0mg**; Total Carbohydrate **2.0g**; Dietary Fiber **1.3g**; Protein **0.3g**

Cajun Essence

Makes ½ cup | *Pictured on pg. 268* | Commercial Cajun seasoning blends are often inconsistent when it comes to heat. Some brands are hotter than others, and the spices used in each can also vary. For these reasons I prefer blending my own Cajun seasoning.

2 tbsp sweet paprika
2 tbsp granulated garlic
    powder
1 tbsp cayenne pepper
1 tbsp chili powder
1 tbsp pepper
1 tbsp dried oregano or
    marjoram
1 tbsp granulated onion
    powder
½ tsp ground nutmeg or
    mace (optional)

1. Combine all spices and herbs thoroughly.
2. Store in an airtight container.

CHEF'S NOTE: *If you want to substitute a commercial blend for convenience, I like McCormick's Cajun Seasoning from their Gourmet Collection.*

NUTRITIONAL INFORMATION (PER 1 TBSP SERVING) Calories **24**; Calories from Fat **5**; Total Fat **0.6g**; Cholesterol **0mg**; Total Carbohydrate **4.9g**; Dietary Fiber **1.9g**; Protein **1.1g**

Berberé

Makes ¾ cup | *Pictured on pg. 268* | Berberé, a spice blend, is a key ingredient in Ethiopian cooking and cannot be omitted. Although commercial blends exist, most of them are very hot and use cayenne pepper as the main ingredient. To keep control over the heat of the dish, I prefer blending a milder Berberé myself. With this spice blend you can safely add 1 tsp to any recipe, but if you choose to substitute a premade blend for convenience be cautious when adding it.

2 tbsp cayenne pepper, or
   to taste
4 tbsp sweet paprika
1 tsp ground fenugreek
¾ tsp ground cardamom
½ tsp ground coriander
½ tsp ground cumin
½ tsp ground nutmeg
   or mace
½ tsp ground ginger
¼ tsp ground cinnamon
¼ tsp ground allspice
¼ tsp turmeric
⅛ tsp ground cloves

1. Whisk all spices together in nonstick skillet and toast over medium heat, stirring frequently to avoid burning.

2. Once the spices are fragrant and smell toasty turn off the heat and use a mortar and pestle to grind down into a fine powder.

3. Store spice blend in an airtight container.

CHEF'S NOTE: *If you like spicy and hot food, feel free to add more cayenne to this blend or simply add more cayenne or hot sauce to the dish.*

NUTRITIONAL INFORMATION (PER 1 TBSP SERVING) **10** Calories; Calories from Fat **3**; Total Fat **0.4g**; Cholesterol **0 mg**; Total Carbohydrate **1.8g**; Dietary Fiber **1.1g**; Protein **0.5g**

Instant Applesauce

Makes 1 cup | *Pictured opposite* | I'm always running out of applesauce in the middle of baking, so I've learned to cheat the system and make my own instantly.

1 McIntosh apple, cored
   and sliced
ground cinnamon, as
   desired (optional)
pumpkin pie spice, as
   desired (optional)

1. Place apple slices in a food processor with 2 tbsp of water and let the motor run until applesauce is formed, adding 1 to 2 tbsp more water if needed.

2. Optional: add cinnamon or pumpkin pie spice for a terrific twist.

3. Store in an airtight container.

NUTRITIONAL INFORMATION (PER ¼-CUP SERVING) ✎ Calories **36**;
Calories from Fat **1**; Total Fat **0.1g**; Cholesterol **0mg**; Total Carbohydrate **9.5g**; Dietary Fiber **1.7g**;
Sugars **7.2g**; Protein **0.2g**

Vegetable Broth

Makes 4 cups | Nothing beats the ease of premade broth or bouillon cubes, but homemade vegetable broth is superior in comparison. It's also a great way to use up veggies that are on their way to expiration. I like to use sweet onions, potatoes, parsnips, turnips, and fresh fennel.

1 onion (any), peeled
1 large carrot
1 celery stalk
3 ot 4 garlic cloves, peeled
1 to 2 tsp yellow miso
4 whole peppercorns
1 bay leaf
fresh or dried herbs (any)

PLUS ANY THREE OF THE FOLLOWING:

1 small brown potato
2 to 4 small red potatoes
1 c mushrooms
1 bell pepper, seeded
1 medium turnip
1 medium zucchini
1 parsnip
1 leek

1. Transfer your selections to a large pot. If using dried herbs, grab each green one you have on hand and give it a good shake into the pot. Otherwise add about 3 to 5 ounces of fresh dill, but any complementary fresh herbs on hand will do.

2. Add 1 tsp of miso or salt, black peppercorns, and bay leaf.

3. Add 8 cups of cold water, or 10 cups if your selections are particularly big.

4. Cover and bring to a boil. Reduce heat to low and simmer until the vegetables are falling apart, about 1 hour.

5. Turn off heat and allow to cool to a warm temperature.

6. Use tongs or a spoon to remove bay leaf and vegetables.

7. Grab a cheesecloth or fine strainer and strain liquid into a plastic container.

8. Cool to room temperature, then store in the fridge for up to three days. After three days, store in freezer in 1-cup measurements.

CHEF'S NOTE: You can omit the miso and add salt to taste for a soy-free vegetable broth

NUTRITIONAL INFORMATION (PER 1-CUP SERVING) ◦ Calories **49**;
Calories from Fat **4**; Total Fat **0.4g**; Cholesterol **0mg**; Total Carbohydrate **10.6g**; Dietary Fiber **2.2g**;
Sugars **4.1g**; Protein **2.2g**

No-Beef Broth

Makes 1 cup | There are a few commercial mock beef broth bouillon cubes on the market, but I find all of them a little too salty for my taste. This is my DIY version.

1 tbsp soy sauce
1 tbsp nutritional yeast
½ tsp Vegan Worcestershire
  Sauce (pg. 272)
¼ tsp granulated onion
  powder
¼ tsp granulated garlic
  powder
¼ tsp ground ginger
⅛ tsp pepper
salt, to taste

1. In a medium saucepan, whisk all ingredients together with 1 cup of water until well combined.

2. Bring to a boil and simmer for 1 minute.

3. If you used water and low-sodium soy sauce, you might want to add a little salt.

> **CHEF'S NOTE:** *If you use this broth in a soup recipe, add a bay leaf during cooking.*

NUTRITIONAL INFORMATION (PER 1-CUP SERVING) Calories **27**;
Calories from Fat **2**; Total Fat **0.2g**; Cholesterol **0mg**; Total Carbohydrate **4.3g**; Dietary Fiber **1.1g**;
Sugars **0.7g**; Protein **2.7g**

No-Chicken Broth Powder

Makes approximately 25 servings | *Pictured opposite and on pg. 268* | Frontier makes a decent vegetarian chicken broth powder, though it contains corn syrup. There are a few commercial mock chicken broth bouillon cubes on the market as well, but I find them a little too salty for my taste. This is my DIY version.

1⅓ c nutritional yeast
2 tbsp granulated onion powder
1 tbsp granulated garlic powder
1 tsp dried thyme
1 tsp rubbed sage (not powdered)
1 tsp paprika
½ tsp turmeric
¼ tsp celery seed
¼ tsp dried parsley

1. Combine all ingredients in a mortar and pestle, then grind into a fine powder.

2. Store in an airtight container, such as a clear glass jar (as pictured).

VARIATION
No-Chicken Broth   ⤸ Mix 1 tbsp of the mixture with 1 cup of warm water to yield 1 cup of broth.

NUTRITIONAL INFORMATION (PER 1 TBSP SERVING) ⤸ Calories **12**;
Calories from Fat **1**; Total Fat **0.1g**; Cholesterol **0mg**; Total Carbohydrate **1.7g**; Dietary Fiber **0.7g**;
Protein **1.3g**

Brown Rice Milk Ⓕ Ⓖ Ⓢ

Makes 3 cups | *Pictured opposite* | The day I found fat-free soy milk was bittersweet. On the upside, I'd finally found a truly fat-free non-dairy milk, but on the downside, it was also highly processed. Later a raw-foodist friend turned me on to homemade almond milk. But I wondered whether I could make homemade brown rice milk. Turns out I can and at a fraction of the price of commercial rice milks.

⅓ c uncooked brown rice
1 tsp vanilla extract
sweetener (such as agave
    nectar), to taste

CHEF'S NOTE:
*You can buy a 100%
natural cheesecloth
at cooking stores or
health food stores.
The tighter woven it
is, the better (mine is
ultra fine). You need
a size that is wide
enough to cover your
container two times.*

1. Bring 1 cup of water to a boil.
2. Add rice and bring to a boil again. Once boiling, cover, reduce heat to low, and simmer until rice is cooked, about 40 minutes.
3. The rice will be soft and waterlogged; drain off any excess water if necessary.
4. Transfer rice to a blender and add 2 cups of warm water.
5. Blend until well incorporated, about 2 to 3 minutes.
6. Add another 1 cup of warm water and blend again. If you prefer an even thinner non-dairy milk, add another ½ to 1 cup of warm water and blend again.
7. Let the mixture sit for 30 minutes. Meanwhile, drape cheesecloth over the top of a pitcher or storage container and secure it around with a rubber band. Make sure the cheesecloth drapes down into the container and is not tightly fashioned straight across, as it needs to act as a strainer.
8. After 30 minutes, use a spoon to scoop any residue off the top of your milk mixture (usually a thin film forms during the cooling process). Once that is removed, slowly pour the milk into the container through the cheesecloth. Be sure not to pour all the bits that have collected at the bottom. »

NUTRITIONAL INFORMATION (PER 1-CUP SERVING) ➴ Calories **80**; Calories from Fat **5**; Total Fat **0.6g**; Cholesterol **0mg**; Total Carbohydrate **16.3g**; Dietary Fiber **0.7g**; Protein **1.6g**

9 Remove rubber band and, while holding the cheesecloth closed, gently squeeze out any last liquid.

10 Add 1 tsp of vanilla extract and 2 tsp of sweetener such as agave, pure maple syrup, or brown rice syrup.

11 Taste, adding more sweetener as desired.

12 Chill for several hours before drinking.

Breadcrumbs

Makes approximately 1 cup | Can't find whole-wheat breadcrumbs at the store?
No problem. All you need is a food processor, a pan, and this trio of steps.

1 slice whole-wheat bread

1. Tear bread into equal pieces.
2. Place in a food processor. Allow the motor to run until the bread is shredded and crumbs result.
3. Place in a single layer on a pan and allow to air out and become stale (should be hard and crunchy).

> **CHEF'S NOTE:** *If you're in a hurry, toast crumbs in a conventional oven or toaster oven for a few minutes at 250°F.*

APPENDIX

Glossary of Ingredients

AGAR FLAKES: Also called agar-agar, this gelling agent comes from algae or seaweed and can be used as a substitute for gelatin.

AGAVE NECTAR: Pronounced ah-GAH-vay, agave nectar is a natural, unrefined sweetener with a consistency similar to honey. It comes from the agave plant, which also is used to make tequila. It can replace honey, sugar, and maple syrup in recipes and works especially well as a sweetener in drinks.

APPLE CIDER VINEGAR: This very acidic and strong-smelling vinegar is made from apples or cider. It is often combined with non-dairy milk to sour it into vegan buttermilk. It's also used for flavor and served instead of ketchup with sweet potato fries. Apple cider vinegar can be found in most grocery stores, but you can substitute lemon juice if necessary.

ARROWROOT: Found at most health food stores, arrowroot is a type of starch that can be used interchangeably with cornstarch.

BEANS: Canned beans are quick, easy, and convenient, but dried beans are more economical. You can substitute 2 cups of cooked beans for every 15-ounce can of beans called for in a recipe. When selecting canned beans, try to buy low-sodium or no-salt-added options. You can find dried or canned beans in most grocery stores, but health food stores have a larger variety and lower prices on organic and no-salt-added beans.

BROTHS: Broths made from bouillon cubes are less expensive than canned or boxed broths, but any light-colored vegetable broth will suffice. You can also make your own (see pg. 278). When possible, buy no-salt-added or low-sodium options.

BROWN RICE: Bran and germ—key nutrients in rice—have been removed to make white rice white, but brown rice is what white rice once was. To save time, stock up on precooked brown rice that reheats in about a minute. You can find dried and precooked brown rice at most supermarkets.

BROWN RICE FLOUR: As the name suggests, brown rice flour is made from brown rice. It's also gluten-free and provides a distinctive taste that lends well to battered foods.

CHICKPEA FLOUR: Also called garbanzo bean flour, chickpea flour is a light-yellow flour made from chickpeas. It's gluten free and provides an egg-like taste in cooking.

CHINESE 5-SPICE: Chinese 5-spice is a blend of spices, most commonly cinnamon, star anise, anise seed, ginger, and cloves. It can be found in Asian markets and the Asian section of most grocery stores.

COCOA: Most unsweetened cocoa powders are accidentally vegan. Hershey's and Ghiradelli are good brands to try.

COLLARD GREENS: These leafy greens are an excellent source of fiber and vitamin C, and they have anti-cancer properties. Collard greens can be found at all health food stores and most well-stocked supermarkets. When preparing the greens, be sure to remove the ribs by running a sharp knife along each side.

CONFECTIONERS' SUGAR: Powdered sugar.

COOKING SPRAY: An aerosol designated as a high-heat cooking spray or an oil-spray can filled with high-heat cooking oil.

GRANULATED POWDERS: Look for onion and garlic powders that are granulated, resembling the consistency of fine salt, and not powders that are similar to flour or confectioners' sugar (the floury spices are sometimes called "California Style").

INDIAN SPICES: Indian spices such as turmeric, coriander, garam masala, cumin, curry powder, and fennel seeds can be found in most health food stores but are very inexpensive at Indian stores and online.

INJERA BREAD: This fermented pancake-like bread is made out of teff flour and is a staple in Ethiopian cuisine. You can purchase injera from your local Ethiopian restaurant, buy it at well-stocked health food stores, or make it yourself—try Google for a recipe.

ITALIAN SEASONING: Italian seasoning is a blend of basil, rosemary, thyme, sage, marjoram, and oregano.

KALE: These leafy greens are an excellent source of antioxidants, beta carotene, vitamins K and C, and calcium. Kale can be found at all health food stores and most well-stocked supermarkets. I prefer the dark, deep green kale commonly labeled "dinosaur kale." When preparing kale, be sure to remove the ribs by running a sharp knife along each side.

KELP: A deep-water sea vegetable that's high in iodine but low in sodium (salt), kelp also gives food a fishy taste and is the key to making vegan versions of fish foods. Kelp usually comes in the form of flakes or granules in a small shaker container. You can find it in the Asian section of health food stores or online.

LIQUID SMOKE: Found in most supermarkets, liquid smoke is smoke condensation captured in water. It looks like soy sauce but smells like barbecue.

MISO: Found in the refrigerated food section of health food stores and Asian supermarkets, miso is usually made from soybeans, although it can also be made from rice, barley, wheat, or chickpeas. Miso has a distinctive salty flavor, therefore lending a great flavor in soups, dressings, and vegan cheese sauces.

MORI-NU TOFU: This shelf-stable tofu can be found in the Asian section of most grocery stores, but it is sometimes also kept with meat substitutes or produce.

NON-DAIRY MILK: Soy milk, rice milk, hemp milk, oat milk, and almond milk are just some of the many kinds of non-dairy milk on the market. West Soy makes a fat-free soy milk, but many other brands make light non-dairy milks that have a marginal amount of fat. These milks can be used interchangeably in recipes, so feel free to use any type of milk you enjoy or have on hand. Non-dairy milks can be found on the shelf or in the refrigerated section of the grocery store. Most supermarkets carry at least one brand of soy milk, but health food stores have a wider variety and are usually more affordable. Bulk retail outlets like Costco often sell non-dairy milk for as little as ten cents a carton. If you are new to non-dairy milk, try several brands and varieties to find your favorite. Sweetened almond milk is a good starting point.

Popular brands of non-dairy milks include Silk, West Soy, Rice Dream, Hemp Bliss, and Almond Breeze. You can also make your own fat-free non-dairy milk (pg. 282).

NORI: Found in the Asian section of health food stores, nori are dried seaweed sheets commonly used in sushi.

NUTRITIONAL YEAST: Also called brewer's yeast and savory yeast, nutritional yeast is a deactivated yeast, meaning it doesn't make breads rise the way active yeast does. Nutritional yeast is a complete protein, low in fat and sodium, and fortified with vitamin B_{12}. It also gives food a cheesy flavor. Nutritional yeast can be found at health food stores and vitamin retailers like GNC and the Vitamin Shoppe. I highly recommend Red Star brand, which can be found in some stores and bought in bulk online.

ORGANIC FOODS: Farmers' markets and co-ops usually have the best prices on organic fruits and vegetables. There may also be an affordable organic delivery company such as Fresh Direct, Urban Organics, Boxed Greens, Greenling, Spud, or Door to Door Organics, that serves your city or town. Trader Joe's and bulk chains like Costco carry a limited amount of affordable organic produce and Whole Foods Market can be affordable if you buy seasonally, locally grown, or its brand of frozen items ("365").

POULTRY SEASONING: Poultry seasoning is a blend of basil, rosemary, thyme, sage, marjoram, and oregano, but other herbs can be included from time to time. Avoid buying powdered poultry spice or chicken spice rubs, which can be salty. Look for a granulated poultry spice or make your own blend using the recipe on page 273.

POWDERED SUGAR: Also called confectioners' sugar, powdered sugar is very fine and powder-like. It usually contains a marginal amount of cornstarch. Alternatively, you can make your own by combining 1 cup of raw sugar with 2 tbsp of cornstarch in your food processor and letting the motor run until a fine powder is formed.

PUMPKIN PIE SPICE: This blend of cinnamon, ginger, cloves, and nutmeg gives pumpkin pie and other pumpkin foods that distinct flavor we know and love. You can find it around the holidays, but some stores stock it year round.

PURE MAPLE SYRUP: Pure maple syrup is a delicious natural, unrefined sweetener that is lower in calories and full of important minerals. While it may be tempting to do so, you cannot substitute imitation maple syrups and pancake syrups without sacrificing taste and quality. Those syrups are made from refined sugars and chemicals and will interfere with baking chemistry. Agave nectar can be substituted for pure maple syrup, but the taste will be different. The best deals for maple syrup are online, particularly when you buy in bulk.

PURE PUMPKIN: Pure pumpkin is different from pumpkin pie mix (don't use that). You want canned pure pumpkin or the insides of an actual pumpkin. In a pinch, you can substitute canned sweet potato.

QUINOA: Although technically a pseudo-cereal, quinoa is commonly treated as a grain. It has a nutty flavor and is full of calcium, iron, and magnesium. Quinoa is also a complete protein and cooks quickly, making it a perfect substitute for rice, oatmeal, and other grains when your time is limited. Most U.S. brands of quinoa have been pre-rinsed, but if your quinoa has a chalky coating, rinse it several times before cooking or it will taste very bitter and soapy. Quinoa bought from the bulk bin should always be rinsed before cooking.

QUINOA FLOUR: As the name suggests, this flour is made from quinoa. It's gluten-free and provides a distinct nutty taste.

RAW SUGAR: Also called turbinado sugar, raw sugar is a natural, unrefined sugar made from cane juice. Raw sugar can be found in most supermarkets but is usually less expensive at health food stores.

RICEMELLOW: Made from brown rice and with the consistency of Fluff, Suzanne's Ricemellow is a healthy and vegan marshmallow crème alternative. You can find Suzanne's Ricemellow in most health food stores and online.

SEITAN: Pronounced SAY-tan and also called wheat meat, seitan is a meat analogue made from vital wheat gluten flour. It can be made at home or purchased premade at health food stores. Tidal Wave is popular brand among vegans.

SPICES (GENERALLY): If you buy nothing else organic, try to buy organic and premium spices. A crappy spice can ruin an entire meal. Whole Foods Market has a wide variety of organic spices for as little as $1.99 each. If you don't mind buying in bulk, specialty spice shops and online shops offer great deals. Good brands to try include Rani, Frontier, Swanson, Spice Islands, Spice Hunter, Simply Organic, Amish Market, and Penzey's.

SOY YOGURT: Soy yogurt is made from soy instead of dairy. Alternatively, there are also coconut milk yogurts and rice milk yogurts. Most supermarkets carry at least one brand of soy yogurt, but health food stores carry a wider variety of non-dairy yogurts and at a lower price.

TAMARI: Interchangeable with soy sauce in recipes, tamari is similar to soy sauce but thicker and usually gluten-free.

TEXTURED VEGETABLE PROTEIN: Commonly referred to as "TVP," textured vegetable protein is a meat analogue made from reduced-fat soy flour. It comes in the form of granules and must be reconstituted in water or broth. TVP is a good source of protein and essential amino acids. It is also called textured soy protein, or "TSP." TVP and/or TSP can be found in some well-stocked supermarkets, but they are always available at health food stores and online.

TOFU: Made from the curds of soy milk, tofu is high in protein, iron, omega-3 fatty acids, and calcium. Since tofu is also colorless and flavorless, it is wonderfully universal in cooking. There are two distinct types of tofu: tofu that is refrigerated and sitting in water, and Tetra-packed tofu, such as Mori-Nu, that is shelf stable. Tetra-packed tofu is very soft and delicate and works best as a creamy ingredient. Refrigerated tofu, on the other hand, can have a much firmer texture, making it a great replacement for meat. There are several kinds of refrigerated tofu: soft or silken, which is delicate; firm; extra firm; and super protein, which is the hardest. The consistency of tofu also changes when it is fried, cooked, baked, or frozen and later thawed. Mori-Nu, Nasoya, West Soy, and Wild Harvest are popular brands.

VEGAN CHEESES: When selecting vegan cheese, it's important to make sure that it is in fact vegan, meaning that it doesn't contain casein or whey. With the exception of vegan Parmesan by Galaxy Nutritional

Foods and vegan non-hydrogenated cream cheese by Tofutti, vegan cheese is optional in every recipe in this book because it is a processed food and typically high in fat. Unfortunately, the soy and rice cheeses at most supermarkets are not usually vegan (they contain milk proteins, such as casein or whey), so make a special trip to a health food store, where there is more of a variety. You may also need to shop around or ask the store to stock certain brands. I recommend Tofutti, Follow Your Heart, Teese, and Daiya.

VEGAN CHOCOLATE CHIPS: Many semi-sweet chocolate chips are accidentally vegan. Ghirardelli is my favorite brand.

VEGAN MEATS/MEAT SUBSTITUTES: The taste, consistency, and quality of vegetarian meats have come a long way in recent years. When selecting a meat substitute, it is important to make sure that it is in fact vegan, meaning it doesn't contain eggs, milk, whey, or casein. Unfortunately, most of the mock meats at supermarkets are not vegan. However, health food stores offer a wide variety of vegan meat substitutes and at a lower price. Smart and Light Life products are also usually fat-free and vegan. Other good brands to try include Yves, Boca, Gardein, and Gardenburger.

VITAL WHEAT GLUTEN: Gluten is the protein found in wheat. It's what gives bread its shape and pizza dough its elasticity. When steamed, baked, boiled, or otherwise cooked, gluten becomes chewy, with a very meat-like texture, and is referred to as seitan. Gluten also works as a binding agent, helping hold things like mushroom burgers together. You can find vital wheat gluten in the baking section of health food stores or online.

Recipe Substitutions

Just about any recipe can be adapted to be healthy, vegan, and fat-free with the right substitutions.

EGG REPLACEMENT: Replacing eggs is often the trickiest part of vegan baking. Thankfully there are plenty of ways to replace them:

REPLACEMENT FOR 1 WHOLE EGG	WHEN TO ADD	CAUTION	WORKS BEST
¼ c silken tofu (2 oz)	Blend with liquid.	Can be very heavy. Do not use in recipes where multiple eggs must be replaced.	in a pinch
½ banana, mashed	Cream with sugar.	Very ripe bananas will leave a hint of flavor and increase sweetness.	in fat-free cookies, breads, muffins, pancakes
¼ c applesauce	Add with wet ingredients.	Avoid using more than 1 cup of applesauce total in any recipe.	in breads, muffins, cakes, cupcakes
¼ c non-dairy yogurt	Blend with liquid or wet ingredients.	Can be heavy.	in brownies
2½ tbsp ground flax seeds mixed with 3 tbsp water	Add as "egg" is called for originally.	Adds an earthy, nutty taste. Can provide firm or chewy texture.	in chocolate recipes, granola bars, oatmeal cookies
Ener-G Egg Replacer	Add as "egg" is called for originally.	Leaves a chalky taste.	for beginners

To replace one egg white, combine 1 tbsp agar powder dissolved into 1 tbsp of water. Whip it, chill it, and then whip it again.

BUTTERMILK SUBSTITUTION: To replace buttermilk, combine 1 cup of soy milk with 1 tsp of lemon juice or apple cider vinegar. Whisk until foamy and bubbly. This soy buttermilk mixture can replace buttermilk 1:1 in any baking recipe.

FAT REPLACEMENT: Applesauce is the most common way to replace fat (e.g., oil, butter), but beans and vegetables also work as a direct replacement:

REPLACEMENT	CAUTION	WORKS BEST
applesauce	Avoid using more than 1 c of applesauce in any recipe.	in cakes, cupcakes, some cookies
pureed beans	Beans add a fudgy texture. Be sure to match your beans with the color of your goodies.	in brownies, oatmeal cookies
canned pure pumpkin	Adds a hint of pumpkin flavor and an orange color.	in muffins, chocolate treats, oatmeal
shredded zucchini	Locks in moisture.	in muffins, breads, chocolate treats
vegan cream cheese	Avoid replacing more than ¼ c of margarine or shortening.	in pastries, biscuits (any time you need to "cut in" fat)
cold banana	Adds a hint of banana flavor.	in scones

SUGAR REPLACEMENT: You can safely reduce sugar by one-fourth in any recipe, or use these other sweeteners instead of sugar:

REPLACEMENT FOR 1 CUP OF SUGAR	ADDITIONAL CHANGES
¾ c agave nectar	Reduce liquids by ⅓
¾ c barley malt syrup	Reduce liquid by ¼
1 c brown rice syrup	Reduce liquids by ¼
⅔ c date sugar	(no reduction)
1 c fruit syrup	Reduce liquid by ¼
1 c pure maple syrup	Reduce liquid by 3 tbsp, add ¼ tsp baking soda
1 c Sucanat	(no reduction)
1 tsp powdered stevia	(no reduction)

Metric Conversions

ABBREVIATION KEY

tsp = teaspoon   **tbsp** = tablespoon   **dsp** = dessert spoon

U.S. STANDARD	U.K.
¼ tsp	¼ tsp (scant)
½ tsp	½ tsp (scant)
¾ tsp	½ tsp (rounded)
1 tsp	¾ tsp (slightly rounded)
1 tbsp	2 ½ tsp
¼ cup	¼ cup minus 1 dsp
⅓ cup	¼ cup plus 1 tsp
½ cup	⅓ cup plus 2 dsp
⅔ cup	½ cup plus 1 tbsp
¾ cup	½ cup plus 2 tbsp
1 cup	¾ cup and 2 dsp

Index

Acknowledgments

The success of Happyherbivore.com and this cookbook could not be possible without the help of so many people.

Scott, you are the most supportive, encouraging, and understanding husband a wife could ever ask for. Glenn Yeffeth and the BenBella family, thank you for making this dream come true. Also, Lisa Barley, an avalanche of good fortune starts with one snowflake; you are that snowflake. Kristen Abernethy Morgan, without you, Happy Herbivore would be a rose by some other name. Talia Levin, Jenni Mischel and Nick Easterling for your unwavering support. My pugs, Quaid and Lily Bean, thank you for licking up everything I drop and spill on the floor. My parents, Richard and Lenore Shay, for teaching me to dream big.

I'd also like to thank Katherine Habr for her photography assistance and Jane Brunk for giving me her dishes to use as props. And again, I thank my husband, who painstakingly reviewed more than 5,000 photos and convinced me they weren't all crap!

Lastly, the amazing group of testers whom I lovingly refer to as my wild chickpeas—I truly, absolutely, could not have done this without you!

Jenni Mischel	*Lisa Harrington Seaman*	*Dewi L. Faulkner*
Diana Dove	*Heather Pare*	*Roxanne*
Katherine Habr	*Lisa Barley*	*Jenny Naes*
Nick Easterling	*Carrie Klaus*	*Mindy Gudmundson*
Lori Maffei	*Tara-Lynn Reidy*	*Sheree' Britt*
Janessa Philemon-Kerp	*Courtney Blair*	
Christina Vani	*Sarah Reid*	

and all of their friends and loved ones who tasted the recipes and offered priceless feedback.

I also hope it goes without saying that I am utterly grateful for the unconditional love, support, and encouragement the fans and supporters of Happyherbivore.com have given me. You light up my life. Everything I do, I do for you.

About the Author

LINDSAY S. NIXON is a seasoned New Yorker, but she was born in Pennsylvania and has lived in Florida, South Carolina, Massachusetts, and California as well. She enjoys recreating traditional foods of the places she's lived in and traveled to, and her recipe repertoire is a melting pot of world cuisines. Lindsay was raised on Polish and Italian staples, but she has a huge soft spot for good ol' American comfort food. Her favorite cuisine to cook is Indian, though she can't imagine her life without Thai or Ethiopian food in it. Adopting a low-fat vegan diet has opened her up to cuisines and ingredients she would have never tried as an omnivore, and it's one of the things she loves best about low-fat vegan cooking—the possibilities are truly endless. It's also changed her life, giving her more energy and health.